TREE GLEE

Other Wellbeing Books by Cheryl Rickman

You Are Enough: Embrace Your Flaws and Be Happy Being You (Vie, 2021)

Navigating Loneliness: How To Connect with Yourself and Others: A Mental Health Handbook (Trigger, 2021)

May You Be Well: Everyday Good Vibes for the Spiritual (Pyramid, 2021)

Be More Wonder Woman: Fearless Thinking from a Warrior Princess (DK, 2020)

The Little Book of Serenity (Gaia, 2020)

The Little Book of Resilience (Gaia, 2019)

The Happiness Bible: A Definitive Guide to Sustainable Wellbeing (Godsfield Press, 2019)

The Flourish Colouring Book: Art Therapy Mindfulness (CreateSpace, 2015)

The Flourish Handbook: How to Achieve Happiness with Staying Power, Boost Your Well-Being, Enjoy Life More and Reach Your Potential (CreateSpace, 2013)

About the Author

Cheryl Rickman is a proud tree-hugger, new woodlander and advocate for the power of nature as a healer and energy-giver. She is also a *Sunday Times* best-selling author and a qualified positive psychology practitioner. Cheryl specializes in writing empowering, practical books to help people fret less and flourish more and is a wellbeing ambassador for the Network of Wellbeing. She owns a small parcel of ancient woodland in the Hampshire countryside with her partner.

You can find out more at www.CherylRickman.co.uk.

TREE GLEE

**HOW & WHY TREES
MAKE US FEEL BETTER**

Cheryl
Rickman

WELBECK
BALANCE

Published in 2022 by Welbeck Balance
An imprint of Welbeck Non-Fiction Ltd
Part of Welbeck Publishing Group
Based in London and Sydney
www.welbeckpublishing.com

A CIP catalogue record for this book is
available from the British Library.

ISBN
Hardback – 978-1-80129-117-0

Designed by Georgie Hewitt
Printed in Dongguan, China by RR Donnelley

MIX
Paper from
responsible sources
FSC® C144853

Note/Disclaimer

Dedication

For Nancy Murillo, a fellow tree-lover and encourager
– I'm planting a Linden tree in your honour.

For my tree-sisters across the globe who share my love
of trees: Iva and Debra, Karen and Helen, Jennie and Lisa, Ann
and Ella, Tanis and Annerose.

For my own tree-climbing daughter.

And, of course, for the trees.

Contents

INTRODUCTION   For the Love of Trees   10

PROLOGUE   Trees & Me   18

PART ONE APPRECIATION

1: APPRECIATE   Why We Need Trees   24

2: SOOTHE   The Comfort of Trees   38

3: SENSE   Sensory Serenity, Survival & Safety   48

4: FLOURISH   Growing the Branches of Wellbeing   66

5: LEARN   Woodland Wisdom   86

PART TWO CONNECTION

6: CONNECT   Connection, Attention & Exploration   106

7: LISTEN   Storytelling   126

8: REMEMBER   What's Your Treestory?   136

PART THREE RECIPROCATION

9: BALANCE   A Harmonious Approach to Tree Care   150

10: ACT   What We Can Do to Reciprocate   162

11: THANK   Thanksgiving   176

CONCLUSION   180

USEFUL RESOURCES   184

ENDNOTES   185

PICTURE CREDITS   192

For the Love of Trees

"Between every two pines is
a doorway to a new world."

JOHN MUIR

While I can't quite remember what I did last weekend, I *can* remember the first time I climbed to the top of the Apple tree in my childhood garden.

I'd hauled myself up to its midway point so often – and sometimes barefoot – I could have done it blindfolded; though I hadn't yet mastered the courage to venture to its daring canopy where its exuberant branches stretched out like wings, probing the sky.

Instead, I would sit on a horizontal branch halfway up, hidden among the leaves, and gaze at the zigzag of branches and the bark spiralling upwards; knowing the promise of a greater prize existed higher up and wondering what the world might look like from up there, amid clouds of green.

My dad, Roger, a carpenter of railway coaches by trade, built me what we called a "tree-house", but was really just an old wooden door that he hoisted up and nailed to that solid branch, giving me a platform on which to sit and eat a packed lunch of cheese and pickle sandwiches, fresh lemonade and a biscuit (or three).

Eating lunch in my tree made me feel a bit like a superhero – doing an ordinary thing in an extraordinary place; and from above. When my friends came to play, I'd often race up to my tree-platform in the time it took one of them to count in Nine-Nine-In (the version of hide 'n' seek that requires the hider to race back to the counting spot while the seeker is seeking). I remember lying flat on the platform, giggling quietly, before scampering down and running back to base.

When I did summon the courage to climb to the crown of this great Apple tree, although a little wobbly, my bold yet small child's heart raced and I gasped in delight as the road to the park stretched out before me. I could see all the way to my friend Lisa's house from this bird's-eye view; see her dad cleaning the car, the washing pegged out on neighbours' washing lines and the mossy roof of our bungalow.

Senses amplified by adrenalin, the hum of lawnmowers and the happy shriek of children playing nearby sounded louder than on the ground. That memory stays with me.

Among these leafy branches in the canopy, I was on top of the world – a

heady mix of feeling powerful yet supported. The tree held me elevated in its strong arms to bring me this precious gift of awe and wonder, and an ability to see further than I'd ever seen before.

I no longer need to clamber to treetop crowns to enjoy their dose of neural medicine. Simply being around and among trees inspires me creatively, lifts me mentally and soothes me emotionally.

I'm not alone in my arboreal admiration. People LOVE trees! Hardly surprising, given we were forest-dwellers and hunter-gatherers long before life became more urban. Feeling connected to the natural world is deeply rooted within our genetic make-up.

Stuck Indoors

Despite this innate connection to nature, we have become intrinsically indoor people. So much so, that in the year 2000, human beings officially became an urban species, with almost 4 billion people living in cities, and that number projected by the UN to rise to 75 per cent of the global population by 2050.

We currently spend between 90 and 93 per cent of our time indoors (and 6 per cent of that time inside cars), and spend more time glued to screens than we spend sleeping; texting, typing, gaming, watching for over eight hours each day, according to UK communications regulator Ofcom.

Stress has been deemed the health epidemic of the 21st century by the World Health Organization. And, while time spent outdoors is on the decrease, anxiety, depression and other mental health illnesses are on the increase; a link we can surely no longer ignore.

Evidently, this divorce from nature comes at a pivotal time – we have never needed to reconnect with nature more than we do today. By staying in we're missing out. In our head-down world, it has become more critical than ever before to look up, pay attention to the natural world and allow ourselves to be nurtured by nature.

Out & About

The good news is we can redress the balance. The Covid-19 pandemic and consequent lockdowns reminded us of the value of getting outdoors. People visited the countryside in their droves; making the most of their permitted periods of exercise away from walls they'd been ordered to stay within.

Pandemic statistics about an increased interest in nature abound. Year-on-year visitor numbers to US national parks rose by between 14 and 50 per cent (depending on the park); plant and wildlife identification apps saw a 60 per cent rise in usage; estate agents reported a significant rise in the purchase of rural and coastal properties; the sale of camping equipment and caravans rose exponentially, as did the number of people taking up outdoor hobbies, such as hiking, gardening and geocaching. All in all, a silver lining to the pandemic's cloud.

The nourishing power of nature is well-documented and widely known now that studies about the positive effects of time spent in nature have filtered through to the mainstream.

A walk-in green space can reduce stress, blood sugar levels and symptoms of depression, and improve concentration, memory and mood. It can boost cardiovascular health, anti-cancer protein production and immune system capability, along with empathy, cognitive function and cooperation. Even simply looking out of a window at trees can make us heal quicker and reduce inflammation and our blood pressure.

Woodland walks or "forest bathing" (a practice based on ancient Buddhist and Shinto practices known as *shinrin-yoku* in Japan, where the term first originated in the early 1980s, see also pages 64–65) are now prescribed by doctors in many countries as nature's own medicine. Meanwhile, Forest Schools have sprung up across the globe as an extension of the traditional classroom.

Slowly but surely, we are collectively recognizing nature's role in optimizing human potential. But what about our role in optimizing nature's potential too?

As a positive psychology practitioner and long-time tree-lover, I've devoted much of this book to exploring *why* trees make *us* feel better and how we can optimize that positive effect by using trees as an essential tool in our wellbeing toolkit. But I also wanted to explore the concept of *mutual* flourishing, of thriving together, because we and the trees rely on each other and have a great deal more in common than we may think.

Mutual Light-seekers

Trees and humans essentially want the same thing – to live good, happy, purposeful lives and to flourish.

A tree's main task is to position its leaves where they have the best chance of soaking up the energy of sunlight so they may, via photosynthesis, add oxygen to the air, clean out pollutants and generate glucose by converting sunlight into sugar.

Meanwhile, us humans, in our quest to boost and sustain our wellbeing, also strive to position ourselves to let in as much lightness as possible, for optimal joy.

Trees and humans are both light-seekers. Indeed, as Florence Nightingale wrote in *Notes on Nursing* (1859):

"It is the unqualified result of all my experience with the sick, that second only to their need of fresh air is their need of light ... It is a curious thing to observe how almost all patients lie with their faces turned to the light, exactly as plants always make their way towards the light."

With that in mind, the aim of *Tree Glee* is to help us find light through the practical nature-based mental health tips and exercises that are featured throughout, while also rekindling our relationship with trees. By learning more about trees and how we can better connect with and care for them, so that they might live well too, we may thrive together.

Rekindling Relationships

To rekindle our relationship with trees and begin to care as much for them as we do for ourselves, we need to deepen our connection to them and our appreciation of them. Only then can we reciprocate in a mutually beneficial way so that our planet can flourish.

Tree Glee is part ode and love letter to trees, part practical wellbeing and nature-connection manual and part call to action. To reflect this, I've organized the book into three key parts:

Part One: Appreciation

Part Two: Connection

Part Three: Reciprocation

Part One: Appreciation

Part One explores our love affair with trees, to uncover what it is about these green giants that stirs our soul. We examine why we need trees, what they do for us and what they mean to us.

While trees provide us with the necessities and joys of life – cleaning the air we breathe, filling us with awe as

we walk through forests and providing timber for the houses we live in, there are deeper psychological reasons for our arboreal admiration that go beyond utility and beauty.

As such, we'll explore the importance of trees and, more specifically, their impact on our mental health, with practical exercises that harness the power of trees to boost our wellbeing. And we'll explore what we can learn from the wisdom of woodlands to help us live life well – from the importance of sunshine and hydration, to stillness, patience and collaboration.

Part Two: Connection

Unfortunately, we have, by and large, grown out of the habit of noticing our habitat. In this part, we'll explore how, by cultivating our curiosity and building our capacity to notice nature and its beauty, we can deepen our connection and develop a stronger relationship with the natural world (and ourselves).

Through a variety of intentional actions, we'll learn how to optimize the gifts trees provide us with, record and share our experiences and rekindle what was once a close kinship.

Taking lessons from the burgeoning Forest School movement, we'll look to wake up our wildness and rediscover the innate curiosity and playfulness we have as children yet, sadly, often lose as adults.

And we'll hear trees' own stories, before digging up our roots to discover our ancient and cultural connections to trees and sharing our own tree tales.

> "Look deep into nature, and then you will understand everything better."
>
> ALBERT EINSTEIN

Part Three: Reciprocation

Finally, we'll explore the variety of ways we can extend our care by giving back to these majestic beings with whom we share this planet.

This part includes a reciprocal action plan and examples of hopeful initiatives that are helping to redress the balance.

The book concludes by returning full circle to the beginning with a "Thanksgiving to Trees" – remembering what Indigenous people have long-known, that gratitude must come first.

But first, I'd like to share my own treestory with you – a tale that took me from appreciation to connection and reciprocation.

Trees & Me

As a child, I didn't appreciate the healing and comforting power of trees, but I soon would.

Mum

When my mother, Denise, died aged 43 of pneumonia and septicaemia, 17-year-old me arrived back to the place where I'd made mud pies, SodaStream drinks and a profusion of happy memories; a place that would never be the same again.

I climbed to my favourite spot in my Apple tree, between Earth and sky, where I hugged the branch and cried heavy tears. I was no longer the care-free child who'd scampered up these branches; life now felt as hard as the trunk I clung to.

For a little while though, the patient stability of those branches gave me comfort. While I crumbled, my tree stood tall, cool, composed – its sturdiness momentarily reassuring.

After what seemed like hours, but was probably just minutes, I climbed down. In that moment, as I journeyed back down to Earth and back to reality, I knew my life would be different without Mum.

Connecting with my tree in that way provided escape and comfort. For, while Mum was no longer here, my tree was – a link back to happier times.

I didn't know it at the time, but I was primed to somehow survive this traumatic event. My parents had given me solid roots and a positive mindset, which, I would later discover during my positive psychology training, would bolster my ability to bounce back. Like my Apple tree, I would endure.

Over the next few decades, a combination of elements slowly healed me – purposeful work, encouragement and love from my husband and friends, walks among trees, and an optimistic and hopeful mindset. Plus, the birth of my daughter.

Flourishing

Since her birth, the trees I've walked among have made me feel good in all kinds of ways. They've made me feel peaceful, joyful and grateful; they've refreshed and relaxed me; they've made me feel connected – to my past, to the present moment and to the natural world. Their constancy and stability have offered me sanctuary and made me feel grounded and protected. They've flooded me with awe at their majesty, and sufficiently fascinated to lead me to learn more about them and how they can help us flourish rather than languish.

I decided to train professionally in the concept of flourishing, and in 2016 I qualified with a Certificate in Applied Positive Psychology. Some topics I touched on during my training resonated deeply with my love of trees – the concept of awe as healing; the character strength of appreciating beauty; and the importance of nature in relation to mental wellbeing and vitality.

Once aware of the significant impact

of nature on wellbeing, I headed up a four-year fundraising project to build outdoor classrooms – to help children flourish; as part of it we created and hosted an autumnal outdoor event called Treefest. Inspired by my daughter, I went on to launch a project called Climbing Trees to encourage children to be proud of all that they are.

As the years passed, I noticed how, whenever I walked among trees, rain or shine, my mood improved, especially when I combined those walks with a gratitude practice. I found the constancy of Mother Nature comforting and noticed that among trees it was possible to grow every "branch of wellbeing", which we'll explore in Chapter 4.

Dad

Now I know the powerful effect trees can have on our nervous system and our capacity to cope, I realize that spending my daughter's 5th birthday in the woods the day before my dad passed away in 2013 gave me a kind of protective balm and the strength to deal with that heartbreaking event.

A week before, dad had asked me to wheel him outside so he could feel the breeze on his face. I pushed his wheelchair probably faster than I should have, but, in that moment, as we whizzed past the tall trees, he looked so joyful and at peace.

The woodland walks that followed his death helped me during my darkest hours. And it's during these walks with the trees that I feel closest to my parents.

Pastures New

When my daughter turned ten, my family and I moved from suburbia to a cottage in the Hampshire countryside. Beyond the back garden lies parkland with rows of Horse Chestnuts; Beech and Lime trees line either side of the house, with a trio of tall Field Maple trees at the front. This makes me feel good. Here are my trees, surrounding me in a protective hug.

Two years after our move, my other half and I took a big leap to acquire some land and manage some woodland. Now, I'm custodian of hundreds of trees, which gives me the opportunity to learn and to deepen my connection to them.

Now, as I enter the afternoon of my life, with trees as my soulscape, I look up at the trees around me and I breathe.

PART ONE

APPRECIATION

Why We Need Trees

"Every green tree is far more glorious than if it were made of gold and silver."

MARTIN LUTHER KING JR.

It does my head and heart good to be with trees. Whenever I walk in woodland I feel at home; my heart expands, my mind lights up and my whole body relaxes. These rooted marvels are my serenity space and sanctuary; trees are my temple, and the forest is my church. And I'm not alone – early gothic cathedrals were designed to recreate the temple of the forest, and *nemus*, the Druid word for sanctuary, comes from the Latin for grove.

As I've discovered in the process of researching and writing this book, this affinity for trees likely stems from an ancestral tug toward nature. Back when human life was inherently bound to the land, it was easier to see the natural world as a gift.

Today, this gift is taken for granted, "taken" being the operative word. There are now half the number of trees on Earth than there were 12,000 years ago, and each year we destroy as much forest as would cover the whole of Belgium.

Thankfully, we can rekindle our relationship with trees and Mother Earth and see the natural world through the appreciative ancestral lens that's long been buried.

A Vital Resource

Rekindling this vital relationship where trees are valued and respected begins with gratitude. As the French explorer Jacques Cousteau (1910–97) said, "People protect what they love." Rather than falling into that human trap of not knowing what we've got 'til it's gone – let's remind ourselves what trees gift and do for both us and the myriad other species that are dependent on them.

Almost half of the known living species on Earth live in forests, totalling 70–80 per cent of land biodiversity; an estimated 60 million Indigenous people depend on woodlands to survive; 300 million people make their homes in forests across the world; and 1.6 billion people work within forests.

It's not only those who live or work in forests who benefit from them. These gentle, generous giants have been way more fruitful than merely providing the fruit, nuts, berries and sap we harvest from them. From apples and pears to actual stairs, in patiently feeding, fueling, medicating, housing and supporting us, trees have helped shape our species, illuminating the way forward, enabling us to climb the heady heights of progress. The materials trees have given us over millions of years have enriched our lives and our evolution as a species so significantly it's difficult to know where to begin.

Timber & wood

The very civilization of humanity has been carved from trees. Indeed, as Colin Tudge says in *The Secret Life of Trees*, in reference to the Stone, Bronze, Iron and Steam ages, and even today's Internet Age, "Every age has been a Wood age."

Trees have given us the timber, tools and scaffold with which to create both great architecture and our simple homes. They've given us the ships with which to explore the world and generously provided shade from the heat of the sun when we arrived on land. Wood has given us fuel to warm ourselves and to smelt with, silk to dress ourselves in, arrows to hunt with and musical instruments and stages on which to perform and entertain each other.

Across the duration of our life, from cradle to grave, trees support us – literally from the Pine and Poplar of the cots we sleep in as babies to the Oak coffins that hold us on our final journey.

Paper

Trees have given us paper to write upon so we may read and learn and grow. Inscribed tablets of Beech wood or vellum leaves bound together made early books and even the word "book" comes from the Anglo-Saxon for Beech, *boc*. Yet, tree-loving bookworms may struggle with their conscience knowing trees become books. Thankfully, the books we read, including this one, often come from sustainably sourced trees especially grown to be turned into paper pulp, rather than from precious old growth. Water and bark from the pulping process is recycled to generate power, ensuring each part of the tree is used and nothing is wasted.

Publishers have even signed a treaty to ensure paper and printing technologies are sustainably sourced, with automated global production of print on demand and other initiatives to ensure environmentally friendly supply chains and carbon footprint reduction in production and distribution.

And well-thumbed books can be recycled back into paper.

Through books, trees provide knowledge, comfort, a means to escape the razzmatazz or doldrums of life. And, just as it's impossible to imagine a world without trees, it's impossible to imagine a world without books.

Healing Powers

Trees help heal our bodies with the remedies that come from their roots, bark, leaves and essential oils, and can help heal our minds with the calming *and* uplifting effects that come from spending time in their presence.

Medicinal qualities

Willow bark gives us aspirin; Cacao trees provide theophylline for asthma drugs; bark from the Pacific Yew helps treat cancer; Pine needles can be used as an anti-inflammatory and analgesic; essential oils from trees can be used to soothe various ailments; and tree shade can help lower the risk of skin cancer.

Seventy per cent of cancer-fighting plants reside only in rainforests and 25 per cent of all the medicines we use today come from the mere one per cent of rainforest plant species that have been tested for their medicinal properties. Trees have so much more to give if we let them live.

Trees make us feel physically better in more ways than we may realize. A 2017 meta-analysis of 20 forest-bathing (see pages 64–65) impact studies[1] reveals trees can improve both cardiovascular and metabolic health. And what trees do to strengthen our body's first line of defence against viruses and diseases is remarkable. Forest bathing increases the activity of our infection-fighting natural killer (NK) cells by 50 per cent and our anti-cancer protein production by up to 48 per cent;[2] an effect which, according to Tokyo Medical University, can last for up to a month afterwards.[3]

Forest bathing can also decrease the inflammatory cytokines associated with chronic disease by half.[4] The woods literally bolster our immunity so our bodies can better protect against infections and tumours. For more on forest bathing, see pages 33–34. Three days of two-hour immersive forest bathing sessions bring the greatest gains, but just 30 minutes of woodland walking each week still brings these benefits.

Even living near trees can make us feel healthier. In one study, New Yorkers who lived near trees self-reported their health as better than those living near other green spaces, such as grassy parks or fields.[5] The same was true for residents of tree-lined streets in Toronto, Canada, whose heart health fared better than those living in a city block without trees.

It's not only our immune functionality which woodland walks improve, but our cognitive functionality too.

Neurological benefits

A widely held belief among psychologists, neuroscientists and other medical professionals about the modern-day mental health crisis is that our demanding, tiring lives mixed with a decrease in time spent outdoors among trees and natural light has led to the stark rise in anxiety, depression and ADHD.

That trees can enable mental recovery and wellness is a welcome solution in providing both prevention *and* cure.

Trees make us feel better by looking at them, walking beneath them and climbing into their canopies. Even looking at photographs of forests and green scenery can have a positive impact. According to University of Melbourne research, even a 40-second micro-break looking out of the window at a natural scene can reduce mental fatigue and restore alertness. A South Korean study of office workers showed those with views of trees reported less stress and more satisfaction.[6]

One study reviewing tree density in relation to antidepressant prescriptions in London found a lower number of drugs prescribed to residents in tree-lined streets compared to those in treeless locations.[7] While a study in Scotland found urban residents living near public parks with trees had lower self-reported stress and cortisol levels than those with no trees or green spaces nearby.[8]

The mental health benefits trees provide explain why Forest Therapy has taken off in countries where suicide rates and depression are highest. Over a quarter of Japan's population, who work longer hours than anywhere else in the world, participate in regular forest bathing.

Korea, which has the world's highest suicide rate, has invested millions into forest bathing, or *salim yok*. As part of their National Forest Plan, South Korea, the first country to offer a Forest Healing degree course, has built a forest healing complex and aims to create "a green welfare state", such is the appreciation and awareness of trees.[9]

And trees can also reduce loneliness. A 2021 Urban Mind app study revealed that when people who live in overcrowded and built-up areas can see trees or sky, their feelings of loneliness dropped by 28 per cent.[10]

The forest effect

Whenever researchers measure the impact of walking in a forest on people's bodies and minds compared to walking through an urban environment, biometric results repeatedly show that woodland walks lower blood pressure, pulse rates, cortisol levels and sympathetic nerve activity, and raise parasympathetic nerve activity, meaning we're less stressed and more relaxed when we walk among trees.[11] Green walks also boost mood and cognitive measures, such as short-term memory and performance ability.[12]

Some survey-based studies run mood profile experiments before and after woodland and city walks, while others hook participants up to measure brainwaves or take saliva samples. Either way, the research is solid: trees make us feel less apprehensive and less stressed.

And you don't even need to walk: in one Japanese field study across 24 forest sites, even standing still looking at trees reduced levels of the stress hormone cortisol in saliva samples.[13] Even leafless trees will do. One mood-tracking Polish study sat participants down for 15 minutes to look at either a bare winter forest with straight trunks or an urban landscape featuring roads and buildings. The winter forest gazers reported more personal restoration, positive emotion, vigour and better moods than the urban landscape viewers.[14]

Forested versus urban walk comparison is important because it shows it's not only that we're taking a break from our busy lifestyles or the benefits of walking that generate these positive effects – it's the trees.

Trees are good for children

Tree time is good for us at any age, but it's especially crucial during early development. A 2010 study of British Forest Schools revealed how outdoor learning and play boost resilience, confidence and concentration, improve behaviour and foster environmental stewardship and an affinity with nature.[15]

Being in nature – or at least outdoors – was part and parcel of my generation's childhood. But not anymore. According to Unilever, prisoners spend more time outdoors than the average child. Sixty minutes of open-air exercise is the minimum recommended amount for prisoners, based on UN guidelines. But 74 per cent of the children of 2,000 parents surveyed spent less than an hour playing outside each day.[16]

Researchers for the journal *Environment and Behavior* found that time with trees has a positive effect on city-based children with attention-deficit disorders.[17] And Richard Louv, author of *Last Child in the Woods*,

calls nature "Vitamin N" and urges paediatricians to prescribe time in woodlands in response to what he calls "Nature-Deficit Disorder".

Woodland adventures, puddle jumping, wood whittling and tree-climbing not only spark children's awe and delight in nature, but according to psychologists at Cambridge University, also enables them to better self-regulate, which is "a better predictor for how well children do later in life than reading and writing".[18]

And when it comes to those educational drivers, connecting with nature has shown to boost children's academic performance too. A recent RSPB study of 775 pupils from 15 UK primary schools, carried out by psychologists from the University of Derby, revealed children who felt a closer connection to nature did significantly better in English and slightly better in mathematics. The nature-connected kids also exhibited higher levels of wellbeing.[19]

Teenagers and those going through the menopause can also benefit, as trees can help alleviate irritability, low mood and brain fog.

Guardians of the Earth

Trees don't just contribute; they are essential to life! Trees are our life force – enablers, facilitators and organizers of life's true essentials – they keep us safe and they keep us alive.

The air we breathe

We rely on our silent companions for the very air that we breathe. Along with the phytoplankton from watery ecosystems that photosynthesize to create half of our oxygen, the three trillion trees on Earth (across 60,000 known species) "breathe" out what we breathe in, as we exhale and inhale in glorious unison.

Every year, each of us is estimated to breathe in the oxygen created by seven or eight mature trees, about 740kg worth!

Trees create air AND they clean it, removing pollutant gases through respiration and by absorbing harmful airborne particles with their leaves and bark. Through this, they help to reduce air pollution-attributed asthma and strokes and heat- and air-pollution mortality. This pollution removal service is invaluable given that 90 per cent of city-dwellers are exposed to higher concentrations than deemed acceptable by the World Health Organization. In London, a 2014 tree survey found that the capital's trees remove 2,241 tonnes of pollution each year. London Plane trees also use their bark to trap and filter harmful pollutants, giving them the nickname, "Lungs of London".

Silver Birch are one of the most effective dust-busters. A study of a street in Lancaster, UK, measured the amount of dust that settled on residents' TV sets before and after the positioning of young Silver Birch trees in the street. Just two weeks later, scientists found that the tiny hairs on the trees' leaves had trapped half of the particulate matter from passing cars, leaving the TV sets 50 per cent less dusty.[20]

Trees reduce noise pollution too – by acting as a buffer, muffling city sounds with their blanket of rustling leaves; a single mature tree can reduce noise pollution by up to six decibels.

Climate-control heroes

Trees cool our homes, cities and planet. Without trees, areas of urban jungle can become "heat islands", up to 12 degrees hotter than nearby tree-lined streets. Trees neutralize this effect, and their heat-shielding abilities can reduce air conditioning needs by 30 per cent in summer and knock 15 to 50 per cent off energy bills in winter.

Meanwhile, humans pump pollutants into the atmosphere, including dangerously high levels of carbon dioxide (CO_2) due to our reliance on burning fossil fuels and methane from farm animals; these greenhouse gases blanket the globe and trap the heat of the sun, causing global warming.

Enter our tree heroes, which, thanks to their impressive "woody biomass", perform impressive carbon-sequestration skills and act as "carbon sinks" to absorb and store the carbon dioxide. A single mature tree can store up to 48 pounds of carbon dioxide in its trunk, leaves, roots and soil per annum. That's as much carbon as a car driving 26,000 miles produces.

Globally, forests and city trees are thought to capture almost a quarter of the total global carbon emissions (hundreds of gigatons), including a third of fossil-fuel emissions, partially righting our wrongs. As such, trees have the potential to save the planet (as long as we stop burning fossil fuels).

Trees protect us further by catching rainwater with their leaves and holding soil together with their roots. They absorb water from excess rainfall to slow down its flow, control erosion, limit flooding and protect ecosystems downstream. They intercept, soak up and filter soil pollutants from our land surfaces, stopping ocean-bound stormwater from carrying pollutants to the sea. And in some areas prolific Mangrove roots stop entire coastlines from being washed away.

Aren't trees super?

The problem is, when forests are destroyed and city trees felled, the stored carbon dioxide gets released back into the atmosphere. And, with continued clear-cutting (when an entire area of forest is logged in one go) and more forest fires, we're losing forests at a terrifying rate, which results in more flooding. See Chapters 9 and 10 for ideas on how we can help save trees (and thus ourselves).

Why Use Wood?

Why use wood at all if their loss is so devastating? Well, as one of the most sustainable recyclable materials available – a low-carbon alternative to plastic, steel or concrete – using wood *sustainably* is better for the planet than not using it.

It's about balance. As Forestry England points out, "Well-managed forests can last forever." Sustainable forestry collects and grows seeds, encourages natural regeneration and old growth, then thins ailing trees to support forest health and uses each timber and wood part so carbon is stored for a longer period than the natural life of the tree.

Coppicing, pollarding and the ancient Japanese technique of *daisugi* also offer sustainable ways of pruning trees to produce more wood from a single tree and result in fewer trees being cut down. *Daisugi*, which only works on specific types of Japanese Cedar, germinates straight trunks of new trees from above the original tree, so the old growth tree remains while the new trees can be harvested.

Tree Valuation

Awareness of source ought to evoke responsibility, rather than continue to take trees for granted. Yet we do.

Scientists have even named this apathy "plant blindness". Too many love trees too little. Perhaps it's because trees make us feel good without us realizing. We simply breathe the air they clean for us and walk on the unflooded earth; we don't hear the noise pollution they've muffled and don't choke on the air pollution they've absorbed. We can't see the carbon they've locked away, so we don't notice these living wonders who make our lives better and easier.

Maybe, to persuade those city and state councils so set on felling rather than managing city trees to factor green infrastructure into their decisions, we need to speak their language of success – profitability?

Well, that's easy enough. The ecological services trees provide would cost billions to engineer. Trees offer exceptional financial value. The London Tree Officers Association recognized this when they came up withCapital Asset Value for Amenity Trees (CAVAT), the first system to assess a tree's value based on its size, health, historical significance and number of people living close enough to benefit from it. The 2015 London i-Tree Eco Project estimated the city's CAVAT value to be £43.3bn.

Existing trees' flood protection and air-pollution removal save billions, while every pound or dollar spent on tree planting yields between five to seven times that in payback. As trees age, they mature in both monetary and planetary value. Surely that's an incentive to retain them in any language?

Healthy & Happy

It is evident that trees are valuable to us and worth looking after because they improve our mental and physical health. But how exactly do trees make us *feel*?

To back up the scientific research, for this book I surveyed hundreds of people on how trees make them feel. I compiled a list of ten positive emotions and asked people to choose and rank the top five emotions that trees made them feel. Serenity and awe came out top, with gratitude, joy and inspiration also placed in the top five.

Respondents also shared other feelings trees evoked. There was the odd "magical", "imaginative", "intrigued" and "inspired", but the most repeated keywords have been grouped into the categories below. Let's call them the 5Rs:

1. **RESTORED:** grounded, calm, relaxed, peaceful.

2. **REASSURED:** safe, soothed, comforted, protected, secure, stable, nurtured, loved, held.

3. **REVITALIZED:** happy, alive, refreshed, satisfied, free, grateful, amazed.

4. **RECONNECTED:** connected, present, whole, home.

5. **RESPECTFUL:** humble, small, accountable.

These responses demonstrate the delicious duality in the restorative effect of being around trees, which both invigorates and relaxes, stimulates and soothes, lifts us up and calms us down.

> "Trees make me feel like I am a small link in nature. How my troubles are small."
>
> JO

> "Trees make me feel insignificant, but in a good way. Like they are a higher power."
>
> JULIET

> "Going into the forest is like going to a temple full of ancient wisdom. It feels serene and peaceful. Always changing, but unchanged."
>
> M BRYANT

> "I feel so secure around trees. They are my friends without legs who always support me."
>
> IWONA

Evidently, trees are a tonic and antidote for many modern-day maladies. But what they give us more than any other feeling is a sense of comfort.

The Comfort of Trees

"One touch of nature makes
the whole world kin."

WILLIAM SHAKESPEARE

Trees' strength and dependability is comforting. Such is their assuredness and solidarity, their constancy and certitude, it's almost as if they whisper reassuringly, "It's okay; we are here." During my research I asked hundreds of people what it is about these steadfast friends that draws people toward them. Over half of respondents mentioned how trees' stability and longevity contributed to their feelings of comfort.

> "I have always found trees comforting. I would often wander out of a party when there were too many people for me, find a tree that I liked, and sit under it for 20 minutes or so before heading back to the party again."
>
> STEPHI

Leaf Relief

As Romantic poet William Wordsworth put it, trees can provide relief from "the fever of the world". Whenever I emerge from underneath the protective branches of a tree, I always feel stronger, calmer, better.

Among trees, the sharp edges of life somehow round off. Whether sheltered from the rain beneath their sprawling branches, leaning against their solid trunks supported by their strength, or walking alongside them, the silent solace they provide gives me a place to breathe in the sweet air of solitude, unfurl my thoughts and think things through. They give me permission to sit in silence, be myself and reboot.

Solace, Space & Solitude

Solitude, especially when surrounded by the gentle rhythms of nature, doesn't feel lonely. Disappearing into the woods alone may disconnect you from other people but, in deepening one's connection to the natural world, it's possible to evoke a kind of "connected solitude" where the trees are your companions. Perhaps that's how trees feel too – standing alone, isolated above the ground yet social under the ground, and therefore balanced.

Trees offer us a place in which to connect with our deepest emotions, to grieve, to question and find answers within ourselves, to tap into our inner knowing. They provide shelter and a soft place to land when we're wrangling with the messiness and challenges of life. They offer peacefulness away from frantic and constant demands. And they help us to remember and honour those who are no longer with us.

The most enduring beings on Earth can act as monuments to lost loved ones – holding memories, marking sorrow and bringing solace to those left behind. There is, perhaps, no better example of this than in Oklahoma City, where a scorched American Elm with debris embedded in its trunk stands tall as part of the city's national memorial to the 1995 Oklahoma City bombing, which took 168 lives. Doris Jones, the mother of Carrie Ann Lenz who was killed by the bomb, told *National Geographic* of the tree, "It comforts me to look at it ... Something good survived something bad."

The Secrets of Serenity

Of all the positive emotions being in the presence of trees evokes, soothing serenity is the most deeply felt. My own research backs this up. In my survey of over 700 people, 74 per cent chose serenity as the top positive emotion that trees made them feel. And two of the Five Rs, Restored and Reassured, (see page 36) relate to trees making us feel calmer.

But why do we feel psychologically and physiologically restored and reassured by trees?

To begin with, woodlands are typically much cooler, shadier and quieter than other landscapes so, as discussed in Chapter 1, stressors such as noise pollution and overt heat are reduced. But there's more to the calming power of trees than escapism and shade.

To understand why they soothe us so, we need to consider how trees engage our nervous system and impact our attention, restoration and cognitive ability.

Trees & our nervous system

Trees make our bodies and minds feel better by producing a glorious cocktail of botanical compounds, which works to soothe our autonomic nervous system and boost our sleeping ability. This makes us feel calmer. These compounds are a blend of essential oils called phytoncides and aromatic terpenes, which trees diffuse between each other to attract pollinators and protect themselves from bacteria, insects and fungi.

When we're walking through the woods, we breathe these in from the woody air and absorb them via our pores. In response to this combination of phytoncide absorption and taking in the soothing sights and sounds of the woodland, our nerves send electromagnetic signals to our brain – specifically to the hypothalamus – which literally flicks the switch to shut down our "flight or fight" stress response and engages the "rest and digest" calm response instead. Our hypothalamus is the part of our brain responsible for maintaining our internal balance or "homeostasis" through heart rate, blood pressure, sleep cycles and emotions; it is the control centre for both stress hormones and happy endorphins.

Switching off the stress response swaps the cortisol and adrenalin production in our adrenal glands for happy hormones such as oxytocin and serotonin in our pituitary glands,

as our calm response is engaged. Our breathing and heart rate slow down, stress and anxiety lessen, so we feel more relaxed and our attention is restored.

According to electroencephalogram (EEG) readings of the brain, in a University of Edinburgh study, nature activates our brains in a way that puts us into a more "open, meditative mindset" and allows for what psychologists call "attention restoration".[21]

Tree-hugging can further increase the flow of oxytocin, the hormone released when we hug loved ones and responsible for emotional bonding and calm.

And if we walk barefoot on the forest floor or sit beneath a tree and touch the earth around us, we release even more feel-good chemicals. The bacteria found in soil – Mycobacterium vaccae – also activate the brain to produce serotonin, a neurotransmitter associated with feelings of happiness, calm and focus and responsible for regulating mood, social behaviour and sleep.

Enhanced sleep

Sleep deprivation causes our sympathetic nervous system activity to increase, along with our blood pressure, while good sleep gives our fight or flight response a chance to relax.

When forest health scientist, Dr Qing Li and the Forest Therapy Study Group conducted a sleep study in 2004, Dr Li found that forest bathing across

2.5-km trails for two hours substantially increased sleep time for the 12 middle-aged male office workers who participated in the study.[22]

The length of the trail mirrored the amount of physical activity they would ordinarily do on a regular day, and the sleep activity was measured using a sleep polygraph and accelerometer (like a counter-Fitbit to define when someone is sleeping).

Their average sleep time rose from 6.38 hours to 7.53 hours on the night of the forest walk, and 7.23 hours the night after. A similar study in 2011 on insomniacs duplicated these results seeing average sleep time boosted by 15 per cent, with the length, depth and quality of sleep improved following afternoon woodland walks.[23]

Better sleep has a knock-on effect to wellbeing. And while better sleep is a key contributor to wellness, so too is exercise, which also boosts serotonin and can contribute further to better sleep health. So, a walk through the forest maximizes serotonin release and both physical and mental wellbeing in one fell swoop. And, best of all, it costs nothing but time.

Trees & our restorative, attention & cognitive abilities

The capacity for forests and parks, tree-lined streets and even images or videos of natural environments to positively change our emotional and cognitive responses has been proven in various studies on "restorative landscapes".

From relaxation to restoration

Between 1984 and 1986, environmental psychologist Roger Ulrich explored the relaxing and restorative impact of nature on how we feel.[24] His curiosity was sparked by drivers going out of their way to drive a scenic route to the mall.

In his famous window view study, Ulrich wished to determine whether rooms with a tree view had restorative influences. He discovered they did: patients treated in rooms with a view of a tree or trees had shorter hospital stays, received fewer negative evaluative comments in nurses' notes and took fewer strong analgesics than matched patients in rooms with a brick-wall view.[25]

Later studies using eye-tracking methods support these findings about the restorative powers of trees, revealing that "natural scenes had a stronger positive restorative effect compared to built scenes". [26] Just as our ancestors needed to quickly recover from stressful experiences and regain composure after being chased by whatever predators they were running from, recovery is important for us modern-day humans. To optimally function in the modern world, we need to be able to cope with and recover from the steady stress of modern urban life.

This restorative effect is why Ulrich wanted to go further than merely proving the relaxing effects of nature. In another study, he decided to see what might happen if he placed the volunteers under stress then recorded how long they took to recover. And stress them out he did!

After showing the volunteers intense and gory videos of woodworking accidents, he measured their blood pressure, heart rates and sweat glands to determine their sympathetic nervous system activity (the system that controls our fight, flight or freeze response). Ulrich then had half the group watch urban scene videos and the other half watch videos of natural scenes featuring trees, with striking results. Those given a fix of nature to view returned to baseline within five minutes. Whereas, ten minutes later, those viewing urban environments had only partially recovered from watching the accidents.[27]

Clear cognition

Trees don't just *soothe* us, they help us focus!

Spending even 20 minutes around trees can boost our memory and concentration, catalyse creativity, and open our mind to problem-solving.[28] In a University of Michigan study, those sent for a walk around an arboretum performed 20 per cent better in a

memory test the second time they took it, compared to those retaking the test after strolling through the city, who showed no improvement.[29]

And the more time we spend replacing tech with trees, the better. Four days of nature-immersion and a decrease in technology exposure resulted in 50 per cent improvement in a creative problem-solving test, according to a study published in the *Public Library of Science* journal.[30]

But *why* does our cognitive functionality improve when exposed to trees? And how does this nature-infused journey from feeling calmer and happier to thinking clearer actually work?

As discussed previously, trees calm us down and lift us up: they both soothe our minds *and* make us feel positive emotions such as awe, serenity, joy and gratitude, among others. And, not only do rested and restored brains work better, but positive emotions also help us think better.

This clarity of thought effect when exposed to trees is threefold.

1. A CALM MIND IS A CLEAR MIND

Calm brains provide access to rational thought, whereas stressed-out, anxious brains don't. With stress, our sympathetic nervous system becomes engaged and our amygdala (emotional brain) seizes control. This means our fight or flight response can flood our brain and body with adrenalin to get it alert enough to deal with whatever we might be about to face, be it real or imagined. This is great for fighting off predators or running fast, but not so good for making rational decisions or thinking logically.

Conversely, when our parasympathetic nervous system is engaged, our prefrontal cortex (thinking, logical brain) takes the reins and our rest and digest response kicks in, enabling rational thought to whizz into action. But the only way to access this logic is to become calm enough to enable the rational side of the brain to take over. Exposure to trees does this, and with immediate effect thanks to the phytoncides they pump out and their power to soothe our senses.

2. A HAPPY MIND IS AN OPEN MIND

The second way trees enable clarity of thought is through the positive emotions we feel in their presence. Positivity has been shown to boost cognitive function and grow our capacity for coping. Conversely, negative emotions can close down our cognitive function, so we become less open to figuring out solutions to whatever we're worrying about.

According to Barbara Fredrickson's "broaden-and-build" theory, positivity literally opens our minds to helps us think more clearly.[31] Positive emotions essentially act as building blocks, which broaden our minds to enable more effective behaviour when responding to trauma and stress. This means the more positive emotions

we feel over time, the more "positivity reserves" we have in our wellbeing store, which we can draw upon during difficult times to help us bounce back better, bolstering our resilience as well as our clarity of thought.

Consequently, the more positivity we can foster as a direct result of exposure to trees, the better we get at navigating our way out of situations that are troubling us. We'll explore ways to ramp up our positivity among trees in Chapter 4.

3. FREEDOM FROM FOCUSED ATTENTION

Finally, trees act as a mind-clarity tool by giving us freedom to think. In today's "attention economy" (a term coined by business strategists Davenport and Beck in 2001), where multiple demands compete for our attention, being around trees give us permission to just be – to rest our befuddled brains, without the need for "focused attention".[32]

Focused attention needs a lot of energy to filter through the many pings, dings and things that demand our direct attention to the task at hand. Being in nature frees us from this energy-draining inward attention, enabling us to engage instead in what environmental psychologist Rachel Kaplan calls "soft fascination", where the landscape gently *entices* attention rather than *demands* it.[33]

I love that gentle enticement of trees, that invitation to "Come, look, be still with us." I always feel more reflective

and more likely to daydream and wonder as I wander in the woods.

According to a 2020 paper published in the journal *Cognitive Research: Principles and Implications*, nature (including trees) offers the optimal amount of stimulation for our brains to rest, compared to focused attention that daily working tasks and even seemingly passive social-media scrolling and TV watching require.[34]

Even better, this freedom from focused attention helps us pay more attention to tasks at hand when we *do* need to return to that focused state. *Not thinking* literally helps us think. And this ability lasts a while. The "involuntary attention" that trees provide empowers subsequent "voluntary attention", so our ability to focus on tasks improves for at least 30 minutes after a woodland walk.

Comforted & Boosted

Evidently, the triple whammy of serenity, positivity and outward attention optimizes our thinking power and helps us find clarity both during and after exposure to a green space – no wonder trees are said to boost our creativity and people report feeling inspired after woodland walks.

Of course, the action of walking itself can have a positive effect on how we feel and think too. However, a study comparing forest bathing with walks in downtown Tokyo showed only the forest environments increased vigour and restored mental fatigue.[35]

Whether the impact of trees is approached from a cognitive perspective (à la Kaplan) or an emotional perspective (à la Ulrich), the two are linked, as the better we *feel* the better we *think* and function.

Researchers know trees have this restorative and relaxing impact by measuring alpha waves, which appear during rest and relaxation, using EEG machines. The increase in alpha waves that occurs when exposed to trees suggests that, rather than being distracted by the constant cavalcade of daily decisions and tasks, or anxious about future possibilities, we have entered the comparatively hassle-free zone of calm.

And there's another reason why trees help us generate such serenity: by triggering our senses.

3 : SENSE

Sensory Serenity, Survival & Safety

"There is always music amongst the trees in the garden, but our hearts must be very quiet to hear it."

MINNIE AUMONIER

How we feel emotionally around trees – serene, comforted and calm – can also be attributed to evolutionary psychology and *sensory* stimulation (what our brains pick up from what we see, smell, hear, taste and touch). Our psychology and our senses are inherently linked.

Survival Instincts

Our sensory affiliation with trees and the comfort they bring have two common denominators: safety and survival; the most primeval drivers for every living creature – be they human, animal or plant.

Senses helped alert our ancestors to danger and enabled them to track a safe passage to find shelter, food and water; tuning in simultaneously to what could harm and hurt us and what could protect and nurture us.

Interestingly, the more we needed those senses, the keener they became. Take snakes, for example. Anthropologists have found that primates who evolved in areas where venomous snakes were common developed better vision than primates who evolved in areas without them.

Certainly, we needed to learn to notice threats quickly. Taking a few leisurely moments to casually consider the beauty of the world could cost our cave-dwelling ancestors their lives. A split second could make all the difference, so early humans needed to respond rapidly to what they saw. As such, their brains were set to high alert. And this tendency to "act (and worry) first, think later" remains.

That overt vigilance has been hard-wired into our human brains ever since danger literally lurked round every corner. It also explains why we have an in-built negativity bias – a tendency to focus on what might go wrong rather than what might go right, and on what's going badly rather than what's going well.

Now that immediate, physical threats are lesser, to optimize our mental health and wellbeing it's important we counter this bias by intentionally "growing the good", which we'll explore more in Chapter 4.

Psychologists studying the speed in which we can categorize natural scenes found that, in less time than it takes to snap our fingers (19 milliseconds), we automatically note the survival features of a landscape, such as shelter, openness, escape routes and temperature.

Breaking the timings down further, researchers found the quickest response came in labelling landscapes as natural rather than man-made, as our brains take longer to recognize more synthetic structures. This suggests we note the naturalness of a landscape before we even properly see the components of it, like a sixth sense or part of our inner-knowing.

Evolutionary psychology

Our negativity bias and our ability to first notice naturalness of landscapes come down to our evolutionary psychology (i.e., how ancient solutions and wiring affects our present behaviour and preferences).

Evolutionary psychology can also explain why tree form has such a deep emotional resonance for us; the reason we feel reassured by trees is because our evaluation of a tree canopy is still based on our evolutionary neural circuitry and our long-held association between tree cover and safety.

We feel comforted by trees because of their dual capacity to both protect us and provide for us. Our neural wiring connects trees to safety, automatically linking to our ancient survival memory. In short, the brain circuitry we've had throughout our existence tells us that trees represent safety, habitat, home.

And our physiology remains adapted to the natural world. Although civilization and urbanization are slowly scrubbing out this memory, we still remember and recognize that everything we need to take care of us exists in the natural world.

Returning home

As you read on, you'll notice the prefix "re" used frequently across these pages – relax, rejuvenate, restore, relief, reassure. The prefix "re" occurs originally in loan words from Latin, either meaning "again" to indicate repetition, or "back" to indicate backward motion, i.e., returning.

And one of the most compelling reasons why trees make us feel calm is the sense of returning home that trees give us.

Going backward may seem at odds with a world so set on moving forward at high speed – progressing, achieving, growing. And yet, returning to our natural roots so we may grow is proving a welcome idea; to replant ancestral seeds in the earth so we may flourish. However, if being around trees restores our mental and physical health, we're not going backward; rather, we're regaining something – connection to the natural world, to our home.

Biophilia

This sense of coming home is rooted in the biophilia hypothesis, which is based on the notion that we feel at home in nature because we evolved in it. Evolutionarily, we've spent 99.9 per cent of our time on Earth in nature, and just 0.1 per cent in civilization. Trees *are* home. As such, our neurons are nature-prepped; they remember this ingrained connection with the natural world, our innate emotional and sensory connection to all living beings and organisms. Trees speak to our primeval brain.

The term "biophilia" was coined by social psychologist Erich Fromm in *The Anatomy of Human Destructiveness* (1973) as:

> "the passionate love of life and of all that is alive; it is the wish to further growth, whether in a person, a plant, an idea or a social group."

This is why our brains, (in addition to avoiding harm by prioritizing fear, pain and threats) also evolved to affiliate with resources that aid recovery from stressful situations so we may regain equilibrium.

Our inner quest to find balance is perhaps why we may seek to escape into the woods when life gets overwhelming or challenging; we may find space in which to breathe and bring the balance back.

Triggering Senses

Our ancient connection to trees is simultaneously a sensory one. And our innate and natural ability to tune in to trees can help restore equilibrium in a rapidly changing world, to bring back a sense of comforting calm.

Sight

Much of our time nowadays is spent staring at screens of varying sizes, but our eyes weren't designed to do this. Experts recommend we look into the distance regularly to counter eye strain and screen fatigue, and that we should also get out among trees often as the sights they offer have the capacity to comfort and calm us.

Fractals

Mother Nature has created natural patterns everywhere – in the veins on the back of leaves, the spirals of unfurling ferns and in the ever-decreasing scales of Pine cones. The detailed botanic arrangements found in the branching of trees, the petals of flowers and the crystallized facets of snowflakes are called fractals – geometric patterns of the same shape that repeat at different scales.

Trunks divide into two branches, which divide into another two, and so forth, replicating the pattern from the biggest trunk to the tallest twiggy branches.

These fractals offer an interesting link between trees and wellbeing, because seeing them has a comforting effect. We enjoy the pleasing visual flow of these natural patterns; they make us feel good and induce some interesting physiological changes in us.

Using an EEG to measure brainwaves of people looking at naturally occurring fractals, even if only for a minute, showed an increase in the production of feel-good alpha brainwaves associated with a relaxed state.

Using MRI scanning to image blood flow and detect which parts of the brain are activated most, physicist Richard Taylor discovered that looking at fractals causes the same parts of the brain to light up as listening to music.

What's more, when Taylor measured nervous system and brain activity by assessing skin conductance, he found we can reduce our stress level by 60 per cent and recover better from stressful feelings when looking at fractals found in nature.[36]

Sometimes these fractals comfort and calm us; sometimes they engage and inspire us in a sense of awe. Whether lulling or lifting, the patterns of trees are feel-good generators. But *why*?

It seems, thanks to having evolved in a natural environment, we find trees' fractals easy to process, using fewer

neurons than we do to take in complex "scale variant" urban scenes and the frequency of stripes.[37] More common "scale invariant" natural features that we are visually fluent in processing create a stress-reducing physiological resonance, which puts us at ease and makes us feel comfortable. Also, it pleases us to look at fractal patterns that match the fractal structure of our own eyes. Nature is cool like that!

And while we're on the subject of patterns, how magical it is that the human fingerprint looks almost identical to the cross-section of a tree trunk; and that the capillaries in our own breathing apparatus, our lungs, resemble the roots of a tree.

Serene green

It's not just trees' patterns that calm and comfort us, but their colour too. Their leaves may change colour in autumn to vibrant yellows, oranges and reds, but we tend to associate trees with a visual feast of greenery.

Natural shades of green reduce stress and nervousness and alleviate anxiety and depression. According to a 2019 study by Qatar University, "walking in a green environment induced a significant reduction in heart rate values [compared to the red and white conditions]." Whereas urban concrete grey can, according to the study, make us feel less calm and more aggressive.

Green can also rejuvenate us. Like nature itself, green has the paradoxical power to be able to both relax us and invigorate us. As 19th-century landscape architect, Frederick Law Olmsted wrote in 1865, green scenery "employs the mind without fatigue and yet exercises it; tranquilizes and yet enlivens it; and thus, through the influence of the mind over the body, gives the effect of refreshing rest and reinvigoration to the whole system."[38]

But is it the images of nature or the colours (or both) that impact us? Keen to find out, in 2012 researchers publishing a study in *Environmental Science & Technology* asked participants to exercise indoors while watching a video of outdoor space. They placed a green overlay over the video for some, a red overlay over others and grey over the third video. They hoped to establish whether the "green exercise" effect could be attributed to the colour as much as the outdoor environment.

Those who exercised in front of the green-coloured overlay were found to be calmer and have less exertion and less mood disturbance than those watching the grey or red overlay. So, the colour green was deemed an important contributor to inducing serenity.[39]

Two years later, more research supported this evidence. According to a report carried out by Andrew Elliot from the University of

> "Green is the prime colour of the world, and that from which its loveliness arises."
>
> **PEDRO CALDERON DE LA BARCA**

Rochester on "mood in college students", natural colours of green can help make us feel at ease when we're in a new environment.[40]

But why does green have this calming effect on our minds and bodies?

1. **Green is a provider.** Green reassures us on a primitive level because, wherever greenery existed there was water, and wherever there was water there was food. We find shelter under green trees, and find berries, mushrooms and other vegetation provided by green plants. This positive association with green is part of our evolutionary psychology, hard-wired into our brains in relation to our very survival.

2. **We've known green the longest.** We're age-old friends, us and green. Human beings have seen greens, blues and browns – the colours of nature – since the beginning of our existence. And we can see more shades of green than any other colour.

3. **Green is on our wavelength.** Green falls in the middle of the colour spectrum, giving it a shorter wavelength, which means it is the easiest colour for us to see as we don't need to adjust our eyes to see it. Falling in the centre of the spectrum explains why green can generate a balanced and harmonious effect.

4. **Green suggests success, optimism and positivity.** Given our in-built human fear of failure (linked to our evolutionary need to survive), anything we associate with success and survival soothes and motivates us. A 2016 study on "Aging and the influence of colour on emotional memories" revealed strong positive associations with the colour green and negative associations with red, perhaps as red is the colour of blood so our response is protective.[41]

Throughout our lives we've seen "ticks" in green and "crosses" in red and, in Western countries, red constitutes a warning to "stop" on traffic lights and green as being "safe" to go. These perceptions filter into our psyche and make green feel motivational, positive and reassuring.

There are only a few negative connotations with green, which are about looking unwell – "green around the gills" – or envy, which originated from Shakespeare's Othello when Iago warns Othello, "O beware, my lord, of jealousy; it is the green-eyed monster which doth mock the meat it feeds on."

As a well-balanced, positive, optimistic, lucky, progressive, environmentally friendly, fresh, hopeful and healthy colour, it's no wonder green is one of our favourite reported colours, second only to blue (another natural colour). And no wonder it has the power to both calm and invigorate us.

Smell

Our sense of smell is primal so our response to certain scents is immediate. A strong sense of smell was critical to our ancestors when food and water was scarce, so scents are quick to enter the primal part of our brain (our amygdala) to which the memory part of our brain (the hippocampus) is plugged in. We are literally wired to remember what smells mean so we can rapidly respond.

Therefore, our noses are sensitive to scent and we can detect over a trillion different odours. During pregnancy, women's sense of smell sharpens as our noses are part of our alert armoury to detect potential hazards.

Tree essence

Trees speak in scent. Aroma is their language. From essential oils to soil bacterium, from bark to leaves, they release soothing smells and comforting feel-good chemicals within us too.

In addition to the immunity-boosting and restorative properties of phytoncides discussed in Chapter 2, the woody lemony aroma of the essential oils released by trees has a comforting and calming effect too.

Aromatherapists have long known the calming effect of trees' fragrances and use essential oil blends from Cedar, Pine, Cypress, Cedarwood and Myrrh to Sandalwood, White Fir, Eucalyptus and Juniper trees to provide a range of benefits (from repelling insects to reducing stress).

Cypress and Pine help stimulate breathing, but also relax us with mild sedative qualities. Studies of NHS cancer patients have shown anxiety significantly decreased while using Pine aroma sticks.[42] The science of forest smells reveals that when the coniferous elixir of d-limonene, g-pinene, β-pinene and camphene are inhaled, it reduces stress by 53 per cent and blood pressure by 5 to 7 per cent as levels of cortisol are lowered. [43]

I can personally testify to the calming qualities of breathing in vapourized hinoki oil from Japanese Hinoki Cypress trees via a humidifier or diffuser.

Evergreen Pine and Fir trees tend to give off the most relaxing scents, but the smell of deciduous leaves, mosses and soil can also calm us. Indeed, the ground does more than ground us; its scent can make us feel safe and comforted.

The aroma of survival (and hugs)

The forest floor, especially when wet, has a particular soothing scent, which even has a name: geosmin. This rich scent of earth after rain is what alerted our ancestors to water sources, and as such it's one that humans can detect even at exceptionally low levels. We used to track it, so we remember it.

Geosmin being the smell of survival explains why it puts us at ease. Physiologically, the scent of the humus on a forest floor has been shown to release oxytocin, the very chemical that is released when we hug someone we love.

And there's more soul-soothing powers in the soil. Mycobacterium vaccae is a soil bacterium that decreases anxiety and increases cognitive ability when we touch it as well as smell it. This is why gardening is so good for us, and why we love a decent bit of damp dirt.

Sound

The sounds that trees, woodland and forests make matter too. Studies have measured and compared the effect of showing projections of a virtual reality forest with or without the forest sounds included. The version *with* sound decreased stress and was more restorative than the forest projected without sound.[44]

And it's no wonder. In the womb, we can hear before we can see. We have a primal affiliation with sounds of nature, which have repeatedly been shown to soothe and relax us more than any other sound – be it a babbling brook, cheery birdsong or psithurism (the wonderful word for the gentle whisper of wind through leaves).

A recent study on the impact of background noise on the brain and body monitored participants' nervous systems, heart rates and blood pressure, as they listened to natural and artificial sounds while performing a cognitive task. Remember the inward attention versus outward attention that impacts our capacity for clarity and relaxation that we learned about in Chapter 2? Well, researchers from Brighton and Sussex Medical school found that listening to sounds from a man-made environment caused participants' attention to be focused inward, the type of attention associated with anxiety and rumination. Conversely, listening to sounds of nature enabled outward attention focus. Furthermore, where natural soundscapes were played, heart rate variability was high and cortisol levels low, proving that listening to the sounds of nature relaxes us.[45]

It hasn't gone unnoticed that Japan – the noisiest nation on the planet (according to the World Health Organization) is one of the most prolific advocates of forest bathing (see page 33). It seems the noisier and more stressful our lives, the more we need the solace that trees provide.

Noise-freedom

Sadly, the world is getting louder with noise lasting longer and doubling in decibels every 30 years or so. Silence has become such a valued and rare asset that Gordon Hempton, an acoustic ecologist from Washington State in the USA who counted less than a dozen local places where anthropone (man-made noise) cannot be heard at dawn for a 15-minute period, decided to apply for a protection order on one single noise-free spot in the middle of the Hoh Rain Forest in Washington State's Olympic National Park. He marked this "one square inch of natural silence" with a red stone atop a mossy log.

Thankfully, trees provide natural silence – a peaceful soothing resource that has become endangered in modern societies where you can barely hear yourself think. Hearing orients us (and wildlife) to our surroundings and alerts us to danger. Conversely, noise pollution disconnects us as much as it stresses us.

And it's not just the trees in woodland that comfort us, the birds that make their homes and sing in them do too. According to acoustics consultant, Julian Treasure, we associate birdsong with the safety of morning. They alert us to the fact that we are here to live another day and reassure us that all is well. Whereas the absence of birdsong alerts us that something is wrong.[46] Even listening to birdsong for just five minutes per day can elevate mood, as natural sounds engage most parts of our brain and make us feel restored. A spoonful of soundscape can be easier to access than meditation.

Safe & Sound

How safe or unsafe we feel determines our level of comfort or distress. Trees, by engaging our senses and connecting with our evolutionary memory banks, reassure us and put us at ease. We can maximize this soothing effect by participating in sensory woodland activities.

As sensory creatures, it's no wonder it feels so good in the wood, with so much uplifting stimulation from immersive forest sounds, sights and scents. But there's more we can do ourselves to make woodland wellbeing last even longer and thereby help us to flourish.

FOREST BATHING

Forest bathing is an immersive experience where you connect deeply with nature as you sharpen your senses or attention. The best place to forest bathe is in woodland with a dense forest canopy, as this means a higher concentration of phytoncides (see Chapter 2); and the best time is either in summer when phytoncides are at their highest, or after rain and during fog when the air is moist.

Most importantly, take your time. The recommended distance to cover is between 2km and 5km, or to bathe between two and four hours, to generate the optimum effect (although forest bathing can positively impact us within just 20 minutes). If you can carve out a couple of hours each month to go forest bathing, your nervous system, mind and body will thank you for it.

If going for longer than an hour, take water to drink and, if there are no facilities (and you are female) take some tissues and a bag in case you need to do a "tree wee"; practicality is important to remove any impetus for frustration.

HOW TO TAKE A MINDFUL MULTI-SENSORY FOREST BATH

- Leave your watch, camera and phone behind, or switch them off. These only serve to distract you and this practice is about savouring the sensory delights of nature through your eyes, ears, nose, mouth, hands and feet. As you let go of time, you let the forest in and, free from distractions, your senses navigate beyond the obvious.
- Step into the forest and pause a moment – notice the trees all around and feel the forest hold you. Feel the breeze on your skin.
- Tune in to your body to allow your intuition to guide you naturally wherever it wants to go.
- Slowly begin to walk and focus on the present moment. Notice your footsteps. Be mindful of your pace and notice how your feet feel as they connect to the earth. At regular intervals, describe to yourself (or those with you) what you can see, hear, smell and feel, and periodically focus on your breath.
- Focus your vision on a single tree. Let your eyes glaze over, look away then let them drift back to cast your eyes over the trunk and upward to the canopy. Tap into that restorative greenery and focus back on the tree. List what you can see: different shades of green and other colours, textured bark, layers of dark fungi climbing the trunk, dappled sunlight dancing through leaves. Consider the luminosity of the area in which you stand. Explore the shadows on the forest

floor and the dark patches between the trees. Can you find any fractals on which to focus your eyes?

- Listen. What can you hear? Tune in to the trees' frequency, the whisper of the wind and rustle of leaves, birdsong, the crunch of twigs and leaves underfoot.
- Place your hands on a tree trunk. Feel the rough texture of the bark, the damp sponginess of moss, the cold smoothness of leaves. Seek out a different tree, perhaps one with smoother bark. Gently rub a leaf between your fingers and notice how each side of the leaf feels: soft, furry or shiny. Periodically crouch or sit down on the forest floor and thrust your hands into the soil. Rub earth between your fingers. Remember, microbes in the earth are nature's own antidepressant. Consider the air around you: does it feel cool on your skin? Is it humid or dry? Is the breeze warm or cold, steady or gentle?
- Sniff the damp earthy soil scent of humus and inhale the piercing fresh scent of Pine trees, the ripe grass and woody smell of trees meeting the earth. Can you smell anything sweet or smoky? Describe what you can smell in the air compared to the aroma of the woodland floor. List forest fragrances one by one.
- Taste the delicate fresh air on your tongue as you inhale those forest phytoncides. Describe the sensations.
- SLUB (Stop, Look Up and Breathe). Play evangelist and leadership coach, Tanis Frame came up with this simple practice to get calm and, together, we coined the phrase 'SLUB' during her Decide to Thrive immersion programme. The premise being that the easiest route to your central nervous system is through your breath. When you pause and raise your gaze skyward, the simple movement engages your ability to inhale and, if you breathe in the forest air as you relax your muscles, your heart rate and blood pressure decrease as you slowly inhale and exhale and sniff the woodland scents as you do so.
- Find a tree that calls to you, lie down on the forest floor and look up at the canopy. Drink it all in. Notice how you feel – relaxed, rejuvenated or both – and how connected you feel to the woodland. Stay there for ten minutes, breathing slowly in and out with the tree. As you slowly rise to standing, feel the difference in your body and exhale.
- Brew and drink tea from pine needles, nettles or blackberries from the forest to complete your immersive experience. As you sip, consider how the trees have made you feel.

Growing the Branches of Wellbeing

"Today, I have grown taller
from walking with the trees."

KARLE WILSON BAKER

In considering how trees impact our wellbeing, it's important to understand what good wellbeing looks like and our own role in raising and sustaining it. What does flourishing entail exactly? And what can we do to boost our level of wellness amidst the trees?

North of Neutral

We've evolved from survivors into strivers. Nowadays, those privileged enough to do so, strive to thrive. Modern psychology has followed this pursuit, developing tools to help us not just cope with life but to flourish and grow.

Until the late-1990s, psychologists busied themselves with helping those who were mentally unwell to become well again; to return from "languishing" to neutral. While this work continues today, in 1998, a new field of psychology arose called Positive Psychology, focusing on discovering and promoting the factors that allow individuals and communities to thrive; to get people from neutral to flourishing, or "north of neutral".

Flourishing is, essentially, optimal human functioning, and the opposite to languishing. Languishing is defined as "the failure to progress or succeed, to lack vitality and grow weak". All living beings and organisms can either flourish or languish – be they human or plant. We can develop, cope and grow well, becoming resilient and ripe with possibility – or not.

What it Means to Flourish

Flourishing isn't only about cognitive and immune system functionality, it's also about how satisfied we feel with our lives and what we can do, practically, on a day-to-day basis to sustain our wellbeing, to keep our life satisfaction levels north of neutral as often as possible.

Researchers have found that, while our circumstances do partially contribute to our wellbeing, how we *respond* to what happens to us has greater impact than the situations themselves.

Psychologist and author Sonja Lyubomirsky studied identical twins and conducted life-satisfaction surveys with thousands of people and discovered that our thoughts, feelings and actions contribute far more to our wellbeing (40 per cent) than the hand we are dealt and the situations we find ourselves in (10 per cent). The remaining 50 per cent of our "life satisfaction set point" – for example, if we have a tendency toward optimism or pessimism – is often genetic.[47]

In general, "even after major setbacks and triumphs" we tend to return to our original life-satisfaction set point. So, when we fall in or out of love, land or lose a dream job, our life satisfaction will rise or fall temporarily, but will then return to its baseline. Positive psychology is about how we can raise and sustain that set point via the interventions we weave into our daily lives to make ourselves feel better.

The Branches of Wellbeing (PERMA-V)

Having researched the key ingredients that comprise human flourishing, one of the founding fathers of the field of Positive Psychology, Professor Martin Seligman, and his team created a mnemonic – PERMA – to summarize the five measurable "pillars of wellbeing" (the foundations of flourishing). I'm going to refer to these pillars as "branches" and they are:

- Positive emotion
- Engagement
- Relationships
- Meaning
- Accomplishment

As with all fields of research and science, ideas and discoveries grow. While studying the mind–body connection, my Positive Psychology teacher, Emiliya Zhivotovskaya, a student of Seligman, expanded the original definition by adding

- Vitality

Thus creating the PERMA-V model of wellbeing.

This sixth branch is as important as the other five, because we can only truly flourish when we are nourished through moving, sleeping, eating and breathing well.

Trees efficiently grow our branches of wellbeing without much action on our part. As we've learned, they can positively impact our physical and mental health in multiple ways just by us being in their presence.

Furthermore, nature connection studies show that *connecting* with trees and the natural world boosts both hedonic wellbeing (our pleasure and enjoyment) and eudaemonic wellbeing (our sense of purpose and meaning). So doing what we can to bolster our nature connectedness can amplify our life-satisfaction. Additionally, by practising positive psychology interventions while we are with trees, we maximize our capacity to flourish.

So, what actions can we take in the woods to feel good?

Positive emotion

Of all the branches of wellbeing, positive emotion has the greatest impact on mental health, improving mood, providing a buffer against depression and anxiety, and countering our inbuilt negativity bias.

It's even possible to boost positive emotions with low-impact ecotherapy activities indoors, as research by University of Wales Trinity Saint David (UWTSD) academics discovered. They found indoor gardening activities instilled feelings of positivity, hope and control in cancer patients who cultivated and cared for their own indoor garden-bowl for a three-month period.[48] While this activity may not be specific to trees (unless growing something a little larger), it demonstrates the mood-boosting power of plants.

Time with trees activates all ten of the core positive emotions:

1. serenity
2. interest
3. hope
4. inspiration
5. pride
6. amusement
7. love
8. awe
9. gratitude
10. joy

We have already explored how trees induce *serenity* (Chapters 2 & 3); and we know trees hold your *interest*, as you've chosen to read this book. Seeing trees simply grow or survive storms can make us feel *hope*, *inspiration* and *pride*. *Amusement* can be found in the funny faces lurking in gnarly old tree trunks and in the tree-climbing or games of hide and seek that woodlands afford. We will consider how trees evoke *love* in the final pages of this book. That leaves *awe*, *gratitude* and *joy*. So let's take a closer look at how trees spark those positive emotions.

Awe

My own research puts "awe" in second place to "serenity" when asked which positive emotions trees evoke.

Awe is a powerful transcendent emotional response to the sight of something extraordinary, from magical forests and magnificent skies to glorious sunsets and panoramic vistas. The unexpected beauty of natural wonders and goodness on a grand scale, whether the majesty of great, straight, towering trunks or the awe-inspiring beauty of leaves changing colour, can leave us spellbound. And being transfixed by trees is incredibly good for us, for the more absorbed we are with nature's beauty, the greater the wellbeing benefits.

In a report in the *Journal of Environmental Psychology* about how "engagement with natural beauty moderates the positive relation between connectedness with nature and psychological wellbeing", researchers found that "the positive relation between connectedness with nature and life satisfaction was only significant for individuals higher, and not those lower, on engagement with natural beauty."[49] So (as we already knew) tree hugging is good for us!

We have a greater tendency to helpfulness when we are awestruck, too. Being inspired by something bigger than ourselves, has been shown to increase "cognition and interpersonal perception prosocial behaviours".[50] Experiencing awe from natural environments may help us to be kinder, more trusting and generous.[51] Trust and generosity levels measured in participants playing games as part of a University of California experiment showed that those who were exposed to beautiful, awe-inspiring scenes of nature before playing the games experienced increased positive emotion, and subsequently behaved in a more trusting and generous manner, compared to those who saw less beautiful scenes.[52]

In another study at the university, those who gazed upward at a row of tall Eucalyptus trees for one minute "experienced measurable increases in awe, demonstrated more helpful behaviour and approached moral dilemmas more ethically", in comparison with those who stared up at a tall building for the same duration of time. The tall-tree gazers also reportedly felt less self-important and entitled than the other participants.[53]

Awe causes our brains to release dopamine, a positive neurotransmitter that lifts mood. So, experiencing awe as we marvel at trees' magnificence can make us friendlier, kinder and happier.

Awe is the opposite of rumination. Awe pulls us out of our own head and back into the world. When we experience awe, inner angst is washed away in a wave of outer wonder. In this way, awe can give our mind some breathing space, allowing us to focus on what we are experiencing in the moment.

Professor of Human Factors and Nature Connectedness at the University of Derby, Professor Miles Richardson, found in his faculty's research into phone use and nature connection that people who were more connected with nature used their phone 50 per cent less, were less anxious, had greater self-esteem and took significantly fewer selfies and more photographs of nature.

There's something else significant about awe as a tool in our mental health toolkit, both in terms of how we view and work on ourselves and how we view the wider world. When we marvel at tall trees and incredible natural sights, we gain proof of the planet's vastness, feel the nobility of something bigger than ourselves, and are reminded that life on Earth isn't just about us. This feeling can generate a deeper sense of belonging and meaning, of being part of something significant, which feels good.

GROWING THE BRANCHES OF WELLBEING

HOW TO EXPERIENCE AWE FROM TREES

GO AWE-HUNTING

Book an excursion to walk a Tall Trees Trail, and marvel at their vastness. In the moment, be awestruck by the sheer size, height and girth of the trees. When you get home, look up corresponding local history and be awed by what those trees might have witnessed when they were tiny saplings.

GET SOAKED ON A WET WOODLAND ADVENTURE

Standing in the rain (in waterproofs!), watching the water pour through the canopy offers a sensory awakening. Being drenched in a downpour with trees around you is awesome. The wet leaves glisten, the raindrops make different sounds dependent on the leaves, and the flood of rainwater pouring down one side of a trunk is a delicious sight. You might return windswept and soaked, but you'll feel so alive.

VISIT A TREE CANOPY WALKWAY

These magnificent structures give us pedestrian access and a birds-eye view from the canopy. Famous walkways include Tahune AirWalk in Tasmania, the 600-metre long and 30-metre high Otway Fly Treetop Walk in Victoria (Australia), Sky Walk in the Monteverde rainforest of Costa Rica, Treetop Walkway at the Royal Botanic Gardens in Kew (England), and Ulu Temburong National Park's forest canopy walkway in Brunei which connects via a series of treehouses and is accessed by longboat.

WRITE AN "AWE NARRATIVE"

After a personal experience of tree-based awe, put pen to paper and relive what you felt, saw, heard, smelt and maybe even tasted. A 2012 Stanford University Graduate School of Business study found those who completed a detailed awe narrative experienced increased feelings of awe, felt less time pressured and had a boosted willingness to volunteer for a charity, compared to study participants who wrote about happy recollections.[54]

Gratitude

People I quizzed in my survey reported feeling grateful to trees for the job they do, for the art of their bark, and for "the way they make me feel like I am loved". Thankfulness is a wellbeing superpower. Alongside altruism, gratitude has proven to be the most powerful and effective positive psychology intervention to boost wellbeing because of its biological impact on our minds. Developing an attitude of gratitude has been shown to literally rewire the neural structure of our brains.

Brain activity studies by the HeartMath Institute and the University of California, showed gratitude practices caused new synapses to grow and neural substrates to build and endorphins to flow, creating an optimal state with "increased mental clarity and brain function". Research shows that those who habitually feel and articulate gratitude perform better, sleep better and see improved heart health and lower inflammation.[55]

It doesn't always come naturally to be thankful though. We need to train our brains to be grateful, because we often forget to appreciate what we've already got. Our default focus is to pay attention either to what we haven't got or to what we wish we had. By regularly appreciating what we have to be grateful for in this moment, we can reprogramme our negatively biased, "survival-based" wiring. And, because gratitude increases the flow of feel-good neurochemicals, such as oxytocin and dopamine, it's been called "nature's antidepressant".

Imagine what happens to your mental set point when you mix nature's antidepressant with nature itself! Focusing on the good while in the woods can bring light to the darkest of days.

Joy

Trees can bring joy in far too many ways to list, but there is one way that is so special the Japanese have given it its own word: *komorebi*, which refers to the joy of dappled sunlight glimmering through leaves. The Japanese language features characters known as *kanji*, and *komorebi* – 木漏れ日 – uses three kanji. The first (木) means tree or trees; the second (漏れ) means to leak through or escape; and the third (日) means sun or light.

There is something inherently magical about this light leaking through trees. Whether during the golden hour as the sun is setting, or earlier in the day as the sun rises, noticing the patterns of sunlight dancing through swaying leaves is joyful wherever in the world we are.

The scientific term for this phenomenon is crepuscular rays, but I prefer the way poets refer to it as "shafts of delicious sunlight" or "windfall light" (Dylan Thomas), or "lances of sunshine that pierce the canopy of a wood" (Gerard Manley Hopkins).

With life's medley of stressors and pressures it's important to practise intentionally noticing the *komorebi* of life. By counting our blessings and savouring slices of goodness, we can counter our tendency to worry and judge, ruminate and dwell. Instead, we can flourish.

GROWING THE BRANCHES OF WELLBEING

FLOURISH WITH THE
KOMOREBI OF LIFE

Become a joy detective. Being a joy detective means hunting for those glimmers of light in life but also in the natural world. Just go out and hone your attention to whatever brings you joy – the shape of a leaf or the beauty of a raindrop on the end of it, the vibrancy of greenery, the feeling of cool grass underfoot, a hopping blackbird, the sound of rain or the dawn chorus.

Record these joyful observations in a list of delight. Then make a second list of the small moments in life that you cherish: from the softness of book pages and the smell of freshly opened coffee to the taste of banana cake or the feel of the dog at your feet. This exercise deepens your appreciation for nature and life, both in the moment and when you read it back. This works well in combination with noting three things you are grateful for. A 2005 study of gratitude journaling showed participants felt happier and less depressed for up to six months after they began the nightly practice of recording three things that went well and why they went well.[36]

Capture moments of delight (or "treelight") by taking photographs of trees that bring you joy. After a challenging week, you can open the picture gallery, look at the trees you've recently captured and realize it wasn't such a bad week after all because there was beauty in it.

Go on a gratitude walk along a leafy lane or through woodland. Walk away from worries and toward creative solutions and appreciation for what you have. As you stroll among nature, say "thank you" in your head for the natural world surrounding you and for all that it gives you, then list everything in your life that you feel grateful for. This offers an alternative to gratitude journaling, and combines the wonder of walking among trees with the wellbeing boost that gratitude provides.

Thank the Universe through a tree. I have a "gratitude tree" whose bark I touch as I list what I'm grateful for and what I hope to bring into my life. I finish with "All is well," and extend my well wishes back to the tree with "May you be well."

Savour real *komorebi*. Whenever you are out in the forest and the sunlight shines through the leaves, pause and soak it up. Step forward and back to notice the different patterns the sunlight casts. Maybe try capturing the beams of light (or "delight") on your camera.

Engagement

You know that feeling where you become so absorbed in an activity that you lose all sense of time? That's the engaged focused feeling of being "in the zone" or finding "flow", which positive psychologists have defined as the second PERMA-V branch of wellbeing.

To find flow, an engaging activity should be sufficiently challenging, but not so difficult that you lose enjoyment of the activity. Adventures among trees can help us feel sufficiently engaged that we achieve this sense of flow.

In his book *Flow*, Mihaly Csikszentmihalyi outlines the criteria or "phenomenology of enjoyment" an activity must have to enjoy flow; we must be able to:

- complete them due to having appropriate/adequate skills
- concentrate on them sufficiently
- exercise control over them
- gain immediate feedback regarding how well we are doing
- forget about everyday worries while embarking in them
- lose self-consciousness
- lose track of time so that an hour feels like a matter of minutes or vice versa

GROWING THE BRANCHES OF WELLBEING

HOW TO ENGAGE WITH TREES & FIND FOREST FLOW

GO ON A FOREST MOUNTAIN BIKE TRAIL

Whether you prefer a lengthy ride or a cross-country, downhill trail to pump adrenaline, or just want to get on your bike among the trees, there are plenty of off-road mountain bike trails at varying levels of difficulty. Search the internet to find the right kind of woodland cycling adventure for you, and always wear a helmet.

CLIMB A TREE

Ensure the tree you climb is healthy with strong branches and sturdy footholds. Avoid trees that have deep cracks, leaning trunks or forked tops, as these features can suggest decay (especially in conifers). Also avoid trees with lots of dead branches on the ground around them or raised roots and fungus around the base as these could indicate a damaged or dying tree.

To climb safely, remove jewellery and wear clothing that won't snag on branches. You might choose to climb barefoot or wear flexible shoes that have good traction rather than hard soles. Climb in good weather that isn't wet or windy. And *never* climb below ominously titled "widow makers": – large branches that are no longer attached to the tree having fallen and snagged.

EXPLORE THE CANOPY

There are professional tree-climbing companies that provide ropes, helmets and guides to help you climb all the way to the top of the canopy. The climb itself is engaging, and the reward of viewing the world from the heady heights of the canopy will likely evoke many other positive emotions, such as awe, gratitude, inspiration and joy.

Relationships

Supportive relationships are a key branch of wellbeing because connections with people who see, hear and support us fulfil that crucial human need of belonging.

Shared experiences bring us closer – from the social bonding that arises from gentle woodland walks to tackling an adventure together in the wild – and is well documented.

To build relationships with others and with trees:

- Establish a woodland walking group. It's a shame, but some women may not feel safe venturing into the woods alone, so finding like-minded people to walk with helps develop connections with others and nature simultaneously.
- Join a tree or woodland conservation group (see page 168). Being part of a community action will bring so many more positive benefits than just forming relationships, and will enable you and trees to flourish together.

Meaning

When motivated to act purposefully – to inspire, to serve, to teach for the good of something greater than our own existence – our lives gain greater meaning. This sense of meaning makes us feel that our lives are significant and important; that they are part of a larger context and therefore make sense. So, the way we actively impact the world is important to our wellbeing, and it can help strengthen our resolve to persist during tough times, because it's easier to have the courage of our convictions if those convictions are meaningful. By finding ways to purposefully help trees via our actions, we can bring more meaning into our lives. See Chapter 10 for a list of ideas.

Connecting with the wildness of woodland can also impact how we make sense of our lives. According to a study in the *Journal of Environmental Psychology*, the greater our level of nature connectedness, the greater our sense of meaning.[57]

Schedule in a period of time in the forest and immerse yourself in nature. A year-long psychological study by John Muir Trust member Michael Wilson suggests this helps us form a stronger bond with the natural world, gain a fresh perspective on the magnitude of the Universe and our own place in it and develop a sense of belonging.[58]

Accomplishment

The fifth branch of wellbeing is accomplishment, because working toward and achieving goals gives us focus and makes us feel good.

By setting goals we stretch ourselves and grow in the right direction – just like trees. And by having a clear target to aim for, a vision to bring to fruition, we put ourselves in control of our lives.

- Plant a tree from seed and feel the sense of accomplishment that comes from growing it to fruit.

- Go on an adventure in the wilderness and prove yourself more capable than you thought you were.
- Set a tree-related goal and devote time to achieving it, be it climbing a tree, finding and recording a set number of different tree species within a certain timescale, embarking on a conservation or art challenge, or planting, painting or photographing as many different tree species as you can within one season or year.

Vitality

Vitality puts the "being well" into "wellbeing"; it's the state of having optimal mental and physical energy, of being alert, active and strong.

Nature is an essential component to our vitality, not only powering up our protection against infection but increasing our energy levels.

In a study carried out on undergraduates for the *Journal of Environmental Psychology* in which half the participants were led at the same pace on a 15-minute walk on a tree-lined path along a river, and the other half on a 15-minute underground walk through tunnels, those walking in nature had significantly higher vitality-change scores.[59]

Similar results were achieved from a green walk-in-nature versus shopping-centre-walk study, carried out in 2007 by the mental health charity Mind UK. "The green walk left 53 per cent of people surveyed feeling more vigorous whereas 45 per cent of respondents felt less vigorous after the shopping centre walk."[60]

So woodland walks and walking in green spaces invigorate and energize us more than walking anywhere else for the same length of time and at the same pace. The benefits are fresh air over the stuffiness of a gym and the sensory appeal of green and the greater sense of space. It may also be because movement around trees feels more natural, less of a chore and more engaging than running round a track or on a treadmill.

Covering All the Bases

Beyond the different practices for improving the individual branches of wellbeing recommended through this chapter, there are some activities among trees that can grow multiple branches simultaneously.

A perfect example of this is adventure, which grows all six branches of wellbeing. A study looking at adventure as a mental health intervention revealed people taking part in adventurous pursuits report feeling more joy, better emotional regulation and quality of life (P), improved engagement (E), enhanced social connections (R), a greater sense of purpose (M) and greater goal achievement (A).[61] And the active nature of adventure ensures it grows the (V) vitality branch too. Adventure therapy, like nature therapy, is now prescribed by doctors in the UK as part of an initiative that enables doctors to refer their patients for mental health and wellbeing support.

The *outdoor* nature of adventure means all the benefits of being in a natural environment apply as well; so adventurous woodland pursuits, such as big tree climbing or forest trekking are a veritable wellbeing win.

Equally, tree-related activities embarked on with other people can grow all six branches of wellbeing, as evidenced by a recent "Forest School for adults" study by the University of Plymouth.[62] This study recorded various wellbeing outcomes, including positive relationship development, purposefulness and feelings of competency. Similarly, as mentioned before, group-based tree conservation work grows multiple wellbeing branches (see pages 81 and 168).

While these may be more time-consuming activities and therefore not provide the quick win that some of the simpler practices can, your engagement in them will bring a wealth of positivity into your life and help you flourish.

HOW TO BOOST YOUR VITALITY AROUND TREES

DO A REGULAR WOODLAND WORKOUT

It's recommended that we participate in physical activity that elevates the heart rate for 20–30 minutes three to five times per week, so why not take your workout to the woods? Use tree stumps for step-ups and strong branches for pull-downs. When working out is fun it doesn't feel like exercise, so make it something to enjoy rather than endure. Fresh air exercise may well help you sleep better too.

STAND ON YOUR HEAD USING A TREE TRUNK FOR SUPPORT

As well as giving you a fresh perspective on the world, headstands improve brain function if done regularly; and MRI studies have revealed that headstands can also improve mood and release stress.

FORAGE

Nuts and berries are an important part of a balanced diet, and it's fun to forage for sloes from Blackthorn, blackberries, elderberries, hazelnuts and chestnuts. Take a nature guide out with you when foraging to make sure you only pick berries (or mushrooms from the forest floor) that are safe to eat.

PRACTISE YOGA BENEATH A TREE

Be it in the woods or in your garden or local park, strike a tree pose to mirror the trees around you. Lift your left foot and place it against the side of your right leg wherever feels comfortable. Reach your hands to the sky and breathe. Repeat the movement, lifting your right foot and placing it against your left leg. We are so often mind-oriented rather than body-oriented but yoga helps connect us both to our *prana*, the flow of life force energy, and to our bodies. Being around trees can induce a similar inward focus. By bringing both together, you can amplify that connection between mind and body.

PRACTISE TAI CHI BENEATH A TREE

Tai chi is a balanced way of achieving stillness within movement while developing your root. A tree trunk, like the human spine, has stability standing upright and still, whereas the branches move gently with ease, achieving strength and softness simultaneously. Be it in the woods or in your garden or local park, as you root down with your feet on the ground, you can achieve that stability. Look up the "Standing Post" move, also known as *Zhan Zhuang*, online to develop this practice.

BREATHE WITH THE TREES

Sit at the base of a tree trunk and align your spine with the tree's spine, it's trunk. The stability of sitting against the tree will help you root down into your breath and be grounded. Close your eyes. Place one hand on your belly and another on your chest. Inhale deeply from your belly and count to four. Hold that breath for four, then exhale for a longer count of seven. Repeat several times. The longer exhale has a calming effect. Open your eyes and shift your *drishti,* your gaze, up to the canopy and gently focus on the leaves as you repeat this exercise. Breathwork can teach us how to breathe better but also how to *feel* better; and not just better than before, but to experience our feelings more deeply. Breathwork can help unblock emotional trauma so emotions flow.

SWAP INDOORS FOR OUTDOORS

For example, you might replace your weekly coffee-shop catch up with a friend with a weekly woodland walk (take a Thermos); or swap the office kitchen to spend your lunch break photographing and identifying trees or having an under-tree picnic. Instead of watching TV, watch the silhouette of trees unfold in front of the sunset. Drink your afternoon cup of tea outside instead of at the kitchen table once in a while. Let your kids climb trees instead of playing computer games to let off steam after school.

Woodland Wisdom

"Trees are sanctuaries.
Whoever knows how to listen
to them, can learn the truth.
They do not preach learning
and precepts, they preach,
undeterred by particulars,
the ancient law of life."

HERMAN HESSE

Quietly wise, trees are a metaphor for living. These silent sages are masters of patience and persistence, they've mastered the art of adaptation and collaboration. They know about the importance of hydration and hibernation and how much there is to gain from the stillness of solitude and the gift of sunlight. Leading by example, their ingenuity extends wide like ancient Yew branches.

Across all species, parents pass their wisdom on to their children – elders teach the young. Trees are no different. Those who've accumulated the most experience of living well share nuggets of knowledge about what's helpful and harmful, secrets of survival shared from generation to generation.

We know that trees remember generational trauma. And when a majestic mother tree is dying, she passes her wisdom on to the next generation of seedlings to bolster their resilience to future threats. Down her trunk and across a woody network, she sends a cocktail of carbon, defence signals and other survival insight.

Yet trees' wisdom is not only reserved for their kin. They have more to teach than who is friend or foe, how to photosynthesize and how to grow. Wise old trees, being some of the oldest living beings on the planet, in their mute green existence can teach us lessons on how to live.

Trees have been here forever; we've only just arrived. We are the students of Mother Nature. So, listen, we must.

> "Trees, ... just as they have longer lives than ours, they are wiser than we are, as long as we do not listen to them."
>
> **HERMAN HESSE**

Collaboration Over Competition

Trees live long lives and grow tall because they operate in a collaborative community of supportive relationships. As such, they remind us that we are better together and can accomplish more when we work *as* one rather than *for* one.

Until recently, prevailing forestry wisdom was based on the principles of Darwinian evolution, believing that individual trees competed for space and resources to survive. In truth, over millennia, trees have developed a healthy forest society built on a vast intricate network of win–win collaborative partnerships.

Trees need each other for survival. A forest that remains intact can create a healthy protective ecosystem, which moderates extreme weather conditions of hot and cold, stores enough water and generates sufficient humidity for local climate consistency. Each tree in the forest community is valued, and unwell trees are nurtured by the other members of the community until they are better.

Trees don't just compete, they cooperate too, giving each other nourishment, support and strength. This is perhaps the most useful and important lesson trees teach us: how to work together in harmony.

Attuned to each other's needs

Good partners stay attuned to each other's needs and mutually nurture each other's wellbeing, which is exactly what trees do. Trees' roots extend and combine with other trees in their community, intertwining for up to 100 feet and connecting trees from one edge of the forest to the other. A single tree can be connected to as many as 250 others via this "Wood Wide Web", a term coined by Professor of Forest Ecology and author of *Finding the Mother Tree*, Suzanne Simard, who discovered that fungal threads link almost every single tree in the entire forest.[63]

This collaboration is key to their survival as, by themselves, unacquainted trees and fungi struggle to live as long. (Simard's research shows that seedlings with access to the fungal network are 26 per cent more likely to survive than those without.) Through these expansive root systems, trees check in on one another, exchange nutrients and relay messages. Meanwhile, trees have formed a network of symbiotic relationships with mycorrhizal fungi, whose tiny thread-like fibres, called mycelium, fuse with trees' root systems, swapping resources to and fro.

The fungi fuse with the tree roots to help them extract water and nutrients (including nitrogen and phosphorus) from the soil, and, in exchange, the tree shares with the fungi the carbon-rich sugars it has made via photosynthesis – a mutually beneficial food and water trade. And, as it requires less energy for the tree to help the fungi's growth than to grow more roots, it's an efficient partnership too.

Weaker trees receive nutrients, carbon-sugar solutions and water from healthy trees via their underground root network. Like a friend popping round with some chicken soup when you've got a cold, trees take care of one another – even different species. Prior to Simard's research, foresters would strip out leafy native understory Birch, Alder and Cottonwood shrubs from the soil so their freshly planted Fir saplings could grow into lucrative conifers without competition. Except the Firs didn't thrive; the saplings seemed more vulnerable to climatic stress and disease with the native understory gone.

When Simard noticed how Pine seedlings surrounded by Alders were thriving, she investigated and discovered that, rather than competing, the Alders and the Pines were collaborating to connect to the nutrients. Inspired by lab studies she'd read, Simard dug deeper and discovered Douglas Firs and Paper Birch were not only exchanging carbon, but the Birch was giving more to the Fir than it received back. The Birch was attuning to the needs of the Fir and generously giving enough for the Fir to reproduce from its seeds. It seemed the more shade the Birch placed the Fir under, the more carbon it donated, aware of what needed replenishing.

Meanwhile, Simard discovered that "mother trees" – the biggest, oldest, and most interconnected – nurture their young. They can determine which seedlings are their own kin and send more food to them than unrelated seedlings, passing the food they produce via photosynthesis to their baby kin whose leaves can't produce enough chlorophyll due to a lack of access to sunlight. They even reduce their own root competition, making space for their children to grow their own roots.

The beginnings of this collaborative relationship go way back and was essential to evolution. It enabled ocean plants and fungi to migrate to land 500 million years ago, where the barren soil and rock needed something to kickstart the process of ecological life. Together, in partnership, trees and fungi facilitated the beginnings of life on Earth.

Harmonious growth & production

The collaboration over competition model that Dr Simard discovered was not restricted to below-ground behaviours.

While trees do race for the light, when they sense a neighbouring tree of a similar height, especially when that tree is part of their closer "inner circle" of family and friends, they stop branching out where the light is already taken and grow where the light is available instead.

Trees also work together to ensure continued tree production. For example, some nut-producing trees (like Oak, Beech and Hickory) buddy up to coordinate when to yield an abundance of nuts and when to produce fewer; they work together to create boom and bust cycles to keep the population of nut-eating animals in check. The plentiful yield takes place every three to five years and is known as a "superbloom", and its effect is that more nuts survive to grow into trees, maintaining an equilibrium between animal and plant life.

> "A tree can be only as strong as the forest that surrounds it."
>
> **PETER WOHLLEBEN,** *THE HIDDEN LIFE OF TREES*

BE MORE TREE: COLLABORATE

CULTIVATE A NETWORK
Develop your own mutually supportive network and check in with each other to stay attuned to each other's needs. Spend time with people who see, hear and appreciate you; and do your bit to lift them up too. Together we rise.

ASK FOR HELP
There's no shame in requesting resources, time, care or support from those around you. People love to be of service, and you can always return the favour when they are in need. That's how supportive communities, like forests, work.

SHARE SKILLS
Consider your strengths, and share those gifts and skills with others in your support network in exchange for learning new skills. Teach and learn from each other. If your friend is a great cook and you have musical abilities, swap cookery lessons for music lessons.

AIM TO ACHIEVE RATHER THAN COMPETE
Trees teach us that growth doesn't have to be visible. We often strive to achieve accolades that can be seen and validated by others, yet we can grow in many ways that aren't always obvious, such as empathy and understanding.

The Art of Altruism

Trees are the ultimate altruists, reminding us that giving is as important as receiving. It doesn't get more generous than making food from water and light thereby sustaining life on Earth for all species, rather than just their own. As Buddha said, a tree even "offers shade to the axeman who destroys it." Some trees are especially altruistic in giving other trees the best start in life. Take Birch, for example, which creates conditions that enable other species to thrive over itself.

Birch trees prepare the ground for new growth by shedding their bark, dropping their seeds and allowing their branches to fall. When birds feast on those seeds, the soil is fertilized with their droppings. Once the soil is good enough for other trees to grow, Birch trees can find themselves shaded out, giving way to enable other species to thrive while they themselves die, fall to the ground and rot, their deadwood continuing to nourish the woodland wildlife.

Then there's dear Alder; these trees are facilitators, creating strong foundations for others. They can help wildfire-damaged forests to recover by converting nitrogen gas back into nutrients in their roots. They love to put their roots down in water, growing in and beside lakes and along riverbanks. In so doing, Alders stabilize the ground along those banks thus enabling other trees to grow alongside them. Similarly, Redwoods offer support to their neighbours during floods and high winds by holding each other up via their intertwined root systems.

Win-win

Of course, the beauty of altruism is that the giver is often rewarded too. For humans, doing good feels good – positive psychologists have long known that when we perform acts of kindness, we get "giver's glow", which boosts our mental wellbeing. For trees, giving berries, nutrients and warning signals means they can facilitate optimal growing conditions for their own families/species and others. A healthy ecosystem enables mutual flourishing for all.

Trees can also offer others protection through self-protection. When under attack, trees pump bitter-tasting repellent tannins into their own leaves to prevent them being eaten. They also exchange messages to neighbouring trees about impending danger (such

> "If you would learn the secrets of Nature, you must practice more humanity than others."
>
> **HENRY DAVID THOREAU**

as invading herbivores), either via emitting ethylene gas or by sending warning signals via their mycorrhizal fungal partners.

They know the favour will be reciprocated, just as their gifts of berries to birds are. In exchange for trees providing berries to eat, the birds poop out the seeds, which return to the earth and grow into trees; a collaborative ecological community built on mutual need.

Trees are not afraid to ask for help when they need it either. If a tree is struggling to generate enough food due to disease or injury, it broadcasts a distress call to the forest who responds by sending sugars to the tree-in-need via the best route in the network.

And trees continue to give even after they have died. The tree roots live on and remain an integral part of the woody community, bringing in water, while the fallen decomposing branches of deadwood send stored nutrients back into the soil; even the hollow trunk becomes a home for an abundance of creatures.

BE MORE TREE: COMMIT TO CARE

CONSIDER YOUR LEGACY

What impact might you have on the wider world after you are gone? What might you be able to do now that could positively impact those you leave behind?

COMMIT TO KINDNESS

Set aside some time to perform acts of kindness. However, rather than performing a single act of kindness each day or week, "chunking" multiple good deeds across half a day or more has been shown to have the greatest positive effect on wellbeing. For example, on reaching the same age as my mum was when she died (43), I carried out 43 acts of kindness to honour her. It took some planning and was tiring, but the warm feeling it brought lasted for days, and turned a tough day into a tender one.

BE KIND TO YOURSELF

Invest in a self-care reward at regular intervals, especially when you're feeling depleted. Nourish yourself with a massage, a meal out, new bed linen, a mini-retreat or an adventure. If your own self-care cup is full, you can pour care into others (you can't pour from an empty cup).

PLANT A TREE THAT YOU WON'T SEE BEAR FRUIT

Our ancestors planted trees that we benefit from today; now it's our turn to pay it forward. As Rabindranath Tagore said, "The one who plants trees knowing that he or she will never sit in their shade, has at least started to understand the meaning of life." (See page 168 for tree-planting guidance.)

Persistence & Resilience

Trees are remarkably resilient. Giant, mature Redwoods, some of the tallest living things on the planet, can range between 800 and 2,000 years old.

The tenacity of trees can be seen everywhere, from polluted cities to windswept hillsides. These ancient beings have weathered the world's most extreme environments for millennia, and frequently experience hurricanes, forest fires, droughts, floods and disease – yet still they stand.

Somehow, against all odds, 170 trees survived the atomic bomb that devastated the city of Hiroshima in Japan in 1945. Many survivor trees' trunks bent but didn't break and these "mother trees" remain in Hiroshima's Shukkeien Garden to this day. Some trees that were destroyed above ground were able to survive, because their roots and underground stalks remained intact, so the trees eventually regrew. In the ensuing years, volunteers and experts lovingly cared for those scorched, scarred trees and, decades later, saplings from some of those *hibakujumoku*, "survivor trees", are sent around the world and planted as "bearers of peace". (Visit www.treeglee. co.uk for more survivor tree stories.)

These trees offer inspiration that what doesn't break us really can make us stronger.

Storms strengthen

In their 2010 research paper, "Whatever does not kill us: cumulative lifetime adversity, vulnerability, and resilience", M D Seery, E A Holman and R C Silver revealed those who have *some* hardships to handle in their lives tend to have higher levels of wellbeing and life satisfaction than those who've had a comparatively carefree life.[64]

Similarly, in their "Authentic Happiness" questionnaire, Professor Martin Seligman and Chris Peterson discovered those who'd experienced adversities in life demonstrated greater acute mental strength and wellbeing than those who had not.[65]

These studies show that – as with survivor trees – experiencing adversity provides us with the capacity to grow stronger, not *despite* of the hardships we endure but *because* of them.

Recent trauma studies have shown that while 15 per cent of trauma survivors developed Post Traumatic Stress Disorder (PTSD), between 60 and 90 per cent developed Post Traumatic Growth (PTG) having reported at least one positive change, such as having a renewed appreciation for life. Further research shows that survivors often stopped taking things for granted, complained less, appreciated

more and no longer "sweated the small stuff".[66]

Evidently, life's hardships can teach us, shape us and often improve us. We certainly learn more from life's challenges than from moments of ease. What's more, each time we overcome an obstacle, we generate evidence to prove that we *can* get through what might have seemed impossible to endure before.

Perhaps this is why trees are so resilient: they endure and they prove themselves. And, just like trees, the more challenges we face, the better we can become at handling what life throws at us.

Adapt & grow

Trees are excellent at adapting to their environments to optimally function.

This might be through their bark, as with the American Beech tree and the London Plane tree. The American Beech first grew in the tropics with rough bark, then evolved to develop smooth bark to prevent epiphytes growing in its cracks. The London Plane adapted to its busy city environment by developing bark that peels so it can discard threatening pollutants.

Or it might be through their needles and leaves. Pine needles resist the cold and retain moisture to survive harsh winters. Some trees, such as the shrubby Bearberry, have adapted smaller leaves so they can bind tightly during cold snaps. And this adaptability can even be seen in indoor plants: the domesticated Weeping Fig sheds its leaves and grows new ones when moved from one room to another.

There is no doubt that trees are masters at dealing with adversity and embracing change.

> "A happy life consists not in the absence, but in the mastery of hardships."
>
> HELEN KELLER

BE MORE TREE: ──────────
BUILD YOUR RESILIENCE

JOURNAL

It might feel hard, but write down some challenges, hardships and adversities you've endured in your lifetime and the strengths you drew upon to get through them. What did you learn about yourself from those tough times?

CHALLENGE YOURSELF

Grow your own grit by setting yourself regular daily challenges where you exceed your previous abilities; this will build your skill level.

TRY NEW THINGS

As often as possible, stretch yourself (skyward like trees). In doing so, your comfort zone will extend, opening the door to greater possibilities.

ADAPT

Don't complain about what you are lacking; make the best of what you have and adapt accordingly.

Have Hope & Embrace Change

Trees are visually explicit examples of changing seasons – the colour, abundance or lack of leaves indicate the time of year and, moreover, the inevitability and constancy of change.

In this way trees are symbols of hope. In her diary, Anne Frank wrote about the Chestnut tree in leaf that she could see from the only attic window not blacked out. The glimpse of "a few small blossoms" gave her a glimmer of hope during a hopeless time. As markers of the perpetual cycle of seasons, trees remind us that, during tough times of scarcity, better things are coming. The knowledge that change is constant can be reassuring – like the harsh cold winter, other difficulties too shall pass. Trees inspire us to go with the flow and trust that current changes will carry us to wherever we need to be. Trees' vivid seasonal transformations provide ample motivation for living life well.

Spring trees – with their newborn buds bursting, green shoots greeting the world, leaves erupting – energize and illuminate the power of new beginnings. Fresh greenery reminds us to have confidence as we bring another year of experience and wisdom into play, and encourages us to welcome each fresh opportunity.

Summer trees' abundance reminds us that good things come to those who wait (and work hard) as their lavish crowns soak up the sunshine.

As the scent of bonfires fill the air and mist stretches across the crisp dawn, in the willing surrender of their leaves to the ground, autumn trees teach us the importance of letting go of that which no longer serves us.

And the bare branches of winter trees remind us to rest and hibernate; to conserve our energy for the coming year.

The importance of rest

During the full flower, nut and fruit production mode of spring and summer, trees send all their energy from root to fruit. Focused, productive and energized, they prepare for this by conserving their energy over the winter.

Sometimes we too need to limit production; to pause, rest and reset

so we can maximize our efficiency, creativity and productivity. Periods of dormancy, of slowing down before rejuvenating, enable us to take full advantage of fresh growth opportunities and possibilities when they arise.

This restful process also serves to protect trees. By hardening off in autumn, trees prevent the water inside their trunks from expanding, freezing and bursting. And by shedding leaves and ceasing chlorophyll production, trees remove surface areas where ice and snow could collect, protecting themselves from a weight of snow that could snap off their limbs.

Such cycles of quiescence are protective for us too. Wrapping ourselves in fluffy blankets, switching off from work demands, and cosying on the sofa *hygge*-style can offer us protection from burnout and stress.

Over winter, trees remind us about the vital importance of rest and recuperation and that there is a season for everything, even downtime. By tuning ourselves to this cycle we can optimally function and flourish throughout the year.

And it's not only trees' seasonal show that demonstrates the cyclical nature of life so beautifully; the concentric rings inside every tree trunk also offer a reminder of these annual cycles as spirals of xylem cells signal one year of growth. A single annum in a tree's lifetime is represented by a light-coloured ring (created by the early wood when growth is at its most prolific) and a darker-coloured ring (created by the slowing of growth toward the end of the summer).

> "Autumn is a second spring when every leaf is a flower."
>
> ALBERT CAMUS, *THE MISUNSDERSTANDING*

The Importance of Being Ourselves

Trees are perfectly imperfect and each one is unique. A scar in the bark, a thick-bottomed trunk, a branch extending at an odd angle; yet they stand proud, boldly taking up space. And they grow stronger with age, accumulating more imperfections along the way.

Trees can't be anything other than authentic. Rather than covering up or diluting who they are to "fit in" (which is exhausting), they unassailably stand upright and stand out, waving their leaves in the wind to say, "Here I am! I am here!" They teach us to stand tall, proud of all that we are, and to embrace our imperfections.

It might feel easier to stay small and avoid taking up space, but doing so can squish confidence. Instead, in being more tree, I can be more me.

> "When the roots are deep, there is no reason to fear the wind."
>
> CHINESE PROVERB

BE MORE TREE: TUNE IN TO NATURAL CYCLES

GO ON AN EVENING WALK

On a clear evening, step out to remind yourself of the natural cycles of life. There is something reassuringly beautiful about witnessing the simultaneous moonrise and sunset; the cycles of life become more apparent – from dawn to dusk, from East to West, from new moon to full moon – cycles of fresh opportunity.

UNBURDEN YOURSELF

What might you need to let go of? A grudge or resentment? An expectation or a toxic relationship? A feeling of guilt or shame? Accepting change shows us that letting go does not have to be about loss, it can be about creating space for the new.

MAKE CHANGE HAPPEN

If something isn't working out for trees (not enough light or water, too many insects) they rectify it by taking action, whether by devoting energy to growing or asking for help. To change life for the better, we too need to act with intent. Changing one small habit can make that shift happen, whether it's waking up or going to bed 15 minutes earlier or eating an extra piece of fruit per day.

HEED YOUR BODY

Think about your natural circadian rhythms of rest and activity. If you are most energized mid-morning, exercise then to boost your energy levels for the day.

TRACK YOUR CREATIVITY CYCLE

Consider when in the day/week/year you feel most creative. I do my best writing first thing in the morning and last thing at night, and schedule my work accordingly.

HIBERNATE

Schedule in periods of hibernation; give yourself permission to wrap yourself in a blanket, light candles and read a book or snooze.

BE MORE TREE
– BE YOU!

CELEBRATE WHO YOU ARE

Use "I AM …" statements and own them, warts and all. For example, "I am hopeful, optimistic and enthusiastic; I am also messy, sensitive and stubborn." Our strengths and weaknesses make us who we are – let's be proud of them.

CELEBRATE AGING

Ancient trees command our respect but what about our own elders? Western cultures make us feel bad about aging, selling us all-manner of anti-aging creams and concoctions to reduce wrinkles and signs of growing older. Yet, with age comes the wisdom of experience and the realization about what matters most. Growing old is a privilege denied to so many. Trees can serve as a reminder of the beauty of growing old and make us feel better about our own aging process as we enter the evening of our precious lives.

CELEBRATE BEING ENOUGH

Choose "enough" over the societal shackles of "should". Instead of beating yourself up for not having done or achieved enough, not looking smart/slim/young enough, not feeling consistently happy enough, remind yourself that making someone smile, being kind or ticking one thing off your list is good enough – then simply ask yourself, "Have I been *me* enough today?"

PART TWO

CONNECTION

Connection, Attention & Exploration

"Instructions for living a life.
Pay attention.
Be astonished.
Tell about it."

MARY OLIVER

Dear Tree

This is an excerpt from a letter penned to a tree. In 2013, as part of a strategy to make it easier for citizens to report low-hanging branches and other such problems in Melbourne, Australia, city officials allocated trees ID numbers and email addresses. But, instead of reporting problems, citizens wrote thousands of messages direct to their favourite trees.

Some trees even emailed back; a Green Leaf Elm wished his pen pal good luck in their exams, while political dialogue ensued between one correspondent and a Western Red Cedar.

Okay, so the city officials may have had some fun with the tree-mail, but the volume of love-filled messages was testament to the depth of feeling citizens have for trees and their desire to connect with them.

> "Dear Algerian Oak, thank you for giving us oxygen. Thank you for being so pretty. You are the gift that keeps on giving."

This reminded me of a workshop I attended a few years ago, run by one of my favourite authors, Elizabeth Gilbert. She tasked us with writing a letter to ourselves from our enchantment (i.e., from our sense of great delight when enchanted by something awe-inspiring). On inviting some participants to read their letters out, a common theme was a plea from enchantment to get out in nature more. If trees could reply, I think they would say, "Come be with us."

Beyond tree-mailing, we can strengthen what researchers call "nature connectedness" – our sense of kinship, belonging and emotional affinity with the beauty of trees through play, curiosity and creativity. And the more connected we feel to nature, the better we feel in ourselves.

What is Nature Connectedness?

While trees are the focus of this book, in exploring how and why they make us feel better, it's important to consider how we experience and respond to nature in general. Ultimately, connecting to nature takes more than simply going outside.

Dr Miles Richardson, founder of the Nature Connectedness Research Group says, "nature connectedness is more important for wellbeing than visiting nature." He and his team at the University of Derby have spent many years researching human–nature relationships to understand what boosts nature connectedness and how that relates to wellbeing. They found that our level of connection to nature tends to be determined by our sense of kinship with the natural world and how engaged we are with nature's beauty. The more we see trees and woods as sources of beauty and awe rather than as mere objects to observe or places to go, the more connected we feel.

What's more, it's not just this emotional affinity that predicts our depth of connection with nature, but our connection to *ourselves*. Researchers found that the greater our level of self-connection, the more predisposed we are to strong nature connectedness.[67]

Self-awareness

Traditionally, research on nature and wellbeing has focused on the practice of mindfulness in a natural setting, because paying mindful attention to forest sounds, sights and other sensory stimuli enhances our awareness and the impact of present experience.[68]

However, new research suggests that the more self-reflective and self-aware we are, the more connected we feel to nature when we're exposed to it. According to Miles Richardson and David Sheffield, "those who tend to take part in intentional self-reflection report greater increases in CNS (Connectedness to Nature Scale) when exposed to natural scenes; whereas those who demonstrate greater mindful attention did not."[69]

It seems that by understanding our inner world and deepening our relationship with ourselves, we can better understand our outer world and deepen our relationship with it.

What's wonderful about this is that while self-connection emboldens nature-connection, the same is true the other way round – spending quiet time among trees facilitates space for self-reflection and can lead us back to ourselves.[70]

Pay attention to self & trees

One Wednesday in September I went forest bathing in my local woods with Sonya Dibbin, a forest-bathing practitioner. As we approached the end of the three-hour session, Sonya led us on a powerful exercise where she invited us to find a tree we felt called to sit with and then to lay down on our rugs beneath our chosen tree.

First, we were going to breathe with our tree – we inhaled the oxygen the tree had created and breathed out carbon dioxide for the trees to turn into sugar and oxygen in this beautiful symbiotic relationship we share. In Persian, "companion" is *ham-dam* meaning "one you breathe with". And here my tree and I were, companions and collaborators in this moment.

As I gazed up at the canopy, I felt a deep sense of oneness with my Beech as she shimmered overhead. But I also found myself attuning more deeply to myself – I could feel the gentle rhythm of my heartbeat, I could sense the gentle breeze on my skin, and I could notice the thoughts my attention drifted toward, before bringing my mind back to breathing with my tree.

In the area of neuroscience and psychological study about interoception – our brain's perception of our bodily state – scientists have found that the more in tune we are with our interoceptive signals, the better we are at regulating emotions and defending ourselves from anxiety and depression.

If you can lay down and breathe deeply with a tree, perform yoga or practise strength training in the woods, this environment can help you tune in to your interoceptive signals, feel more aligned to your innate inner wisdom and more in control of your life. By feeling *physiological* reactions to stimuli, such as a quickening of heartbeat, stomach clenching, breath bracing or muscles tensing, you are better able to feel your *emotions* and regulate them.

In our session in the woods, we were invited to open space within ourselves for listening and ask for strength and guidance with something in our lives we might need help with. Sonya suggested we stay open to the possibility of where that guidance might come from – we might be listening to the tree's wisdom (as is the Druidry belief) or, having given ourself the serenity required, to our own intuition.

I tuned in to my intuition and the tree's resonance and heard "where you're meant to be". This wisdom felt right and appropriate as I'd been questioning a decision made, and now felt supported in that decision.

Later, as I reflected on my time in the forest that day (an important part of the post forest-bathing process is to capture and store the wisdom gained and the feelings felt), I paid more attention to my feelings, leant into what they might be signalling and heeded some internal clues I ordinarily would've missed.

Environ-Mental Health

As both the mental health crisis and the climate crisis expand, a prescription of both enviro-care and self-care has become more critical than ever before. Nature connection gives us a way to tackle both crises simultaneously – a preventative medicine to better connect with and heal ourselves *and* our world.

The Nature Connectedness Research Group has come up with five pathways to nature connectedness (senses, emotion, beauty, meaning and compassion) which, when combined with the UK National Health Service's Five Steps to Mental Wellbeing (Connect with other people, Be physically active, Learn new skills, Give to others, Pay attention to the present) can provide a blueprint to help us move from nature observer to connector.

Exploring these, I've combined this mixture of pathways to nature connectedness and mental wellbeing to come up with three key methods to help us boost our sense of kinship, belonging and emotional affinity with trees and to feel better as a result.

- Notice
- Note
- Share

Notice

Once you cultivate your capacity to notice, you start noticing *everything*. From the way that in the same wind some trees rustle gently and some shake fiercely, while others just shimmer. Or the way sunlight, when it hits dark green Pines turns them into a vibrant sea of colour. And, when you stay in one place, you notice even more.

Sit spot

Revisiting the same spot time after time is, according to leading naturalists, the best way to connect deeply with nature and a good foundation for learning. You can do this by practising the sit spot exercise (see page 112), which is about what's going on *around* a tree, rather than noticing the tree itself. According to naturalist Jon Young, who visited his own sit spot in a forest in New Jersey almost every single day for seven years, "It's not about the quality of the spot; it's about the quality of attention within it." When we pay enough attention, even the most urban spot can teem with wildlife.

Over time, sitting still under a tree self-reflecting will build your self-awareness, your nature connectedness *and* your wellbeing. You will create new habitual neural pathways of noticing, both what's going on around you by paying attention to external stimuli using your senses and to what's going on within you by tuning in to internal cues with your intuition.

THE SIT SPOT EXERCISE

- Find a place under, beside or close to a tree that you will be able to visit regularly and stay with for at least 15 minutes. The tree may be in your garden, a woodland, a park or an office courtyard. Make the commitment by marking "sit spot" in your calendar at regular periods, be it daily, weekly or monthly.
- Settle into your surroundings and notice what sparks your curiosity and sense of wonder. Tune in to faraway and nearby sounds. Sniff the air around you. Extend your vision to detect movement at its periphery edge. My forest-bathing teacher suggests we "orient toward joy" in our bid to get closer to nature. So, if there are flowers nearby, smell them, touch the forest floor and feel the textures. Slowly take in every detail of what you can experience from your sit spot.
- Pay attention to the birds who visit. If you sit in your spot for long enough, you'll be able to decipher their songs. They might be warning others of danger, or they might be giving the all clear. Get attuned to the different tones birds use. You might even try imitating the bird calls, responding to their whistles to deepen the connection.
- Visit your sit spot at different times of day: at sunrise, sunset and in between. Visit during different seasons, during different weather conditions. This way you'll get to observe the journeys wildlife take up, down and around the tree. You'll bear witness to which birds visit your tree and when. And, in time, you'll get to know your tree's home intimately. As you sit unobtrusively in stillness, the natural world will go about its business as if you weren't there. You'll become part of the scenery and able to see, hear and connect with more than you thought possible. Each time you leave, you'll have deepened your connection.
- Focus your attention on yourself for a moment to balance nature-awareness with self-awareness. As you sit, notice what you are thinking and feeling. Can you spot any thought patterns about hopes or concerns? What rises to the surface?
- Uncover what feels true for you. The word "tree" comes from the same root word as "truth". Proto-Indo-European *dreu* or *deru* means firm, solid, steadfast. Ask yourself: "What is my truth? What matters most? To what do I remain steadfast?" Knowing these truths, ask yourself: "What's my next step? Is this decision aligned?" The answers might unlock a way forward.

Notice your neighbourhood

We needn't wait until we're in the rural countryside to notice the trees around us. What's under your nose now – in your garden, street, park, local woods?

Investigating trees in your local area cultivates curiosity, which helps you "Pay attention" and "Learn", two of the Five Steps to Mental Wellbeing (see page 111). And this tree-detective work also helps us to attribute "Meaning" and "Compassion" to local trees and sense our place in the world alongside them, boosting our sense of kinship and interconnectedness.

So, take a walk outside. Tune in to your senses. What captures your attention? Walk round the block and notice which species of trees are the most common in your local streets. Use a field guide or plant ID app (e.g., the LeafSnap-Plant Identification app) to identify trees by their bark, leaves, buds, berries and flowers. Name the three trees that grow nearest to the front door of your home? Do they produce fruits or seeds? Which birds or animals feed from or nest in those trees? Can you discover who planted these trees and how old they are? In particular, befriend a specific tree you can visit often, and get to know them well (see page 116).

Consider mapping your local area. Start by drawing a square to represent where you live, and mark true north on the map using a compass. Then draw an arrow in the direction of the nearest woodland to your home; add another

arrow to indicate where the closest park is. Plot on the map any trees or wildlife that have caught your attention, and each time you venture out look out for new ones to add.

You can either choose to take the same route each time – the ritual and routine of repeating the same movements soothes our nervous system – or you can take an alternative route to expand your awareness and tune in to your curiosity mindset to connect more deeply with your surroundings. You could even flip a coin to decide whether to turn left or right and use a GPS to help you find your way back. See how much more you learn about the trees and your local area using this approach.

Look up what happens to the tree species near you during each season and record your findings. Download the Woodland Trust's Nature Calendar to find out the seasonal cycle of different species, such as when they first leaf, flower and fruit, when their budburst begins and when their first autumn tinting starts.

Perhaps venture a little bit further than your feet can take you and go on day trips to visit local noteworthy trees that may have a historical significance. For example, I discovered that a mere five-minute drive from my home is one of the largest collections of "champion" trees – the tallest, widest, oldest of their species – in the British Isles, at the Sir Harold Hillier Arboretum. As I dug deeper to research trees in my local area, I also learned about a 1,000-year-old Oak nearby and an ancient Yew in a churchyard I regularly drive past.

If you find a troubled tree – a leaf riddled with greenfly, a trunk scarred by deer, a tree that has fallen in a storm –consider how we're not alone in enduring life's hardships. Every living thing has its own challenges; this realization can be comforting and unifying.

And don't stop noticing when you're at home. Throughout the day, whenever you stop to look down at your phone, counter that by looking up and out of the window. Write down whatever you notice: a buzzy hoverfly, pigeons, an ant, a leaf falling to the ground. Each time we notice seemingly insignificant details we flex our noticing muscles and get better at paying attention to the present moment.

CONNECTION, ATTENTION & EXPLORATION

HOW TO BEFRIEND A TREE

- Find a tree you feel drawn to; consider why you felt a connection to this tree in particular. There's a tree I instantly fell in love with as soon as I saw her – a tall slender Yew on which I carved a heart and named the "love tree". The first time I took my then six-year-old daughter to the woodland where it stands, I asked her to guess which tree I'd chosen as our tree, and she immediately ran over to the Yew (she clearly has that effect on people). While researching this book, I visited my love tree after three years of absence. It was like being reunited with an old friend. Being back in those woods rekindled the feeling I used to have when I lived and walked there. Fond memories evoked, I could feel joy in my body as the connection to nature reconnected me to myself.

- Get to know your tree. Examine the bark, feel the leaves. Look closely at moss or ivy growing up her trunk, examine them. Do any animal tracks or trails lead to and from the tree? Are there any holes in which animals may live? Notice any pools of water collecting in bent branches where insects may breed and feed. Pay attention to which insects, birds, caterpillars have made this tree their home. Who does your tree support? Who feeds on her berries, leaves and nuts and builds nests in her branches? Give your tree a good hug, sniff the scents she gives off. Absorb the sounds and sights as you look up into the branches.

- Photograph your tree; ask permission to take a piece of fallen bark or a leaf as a souvenir and give something in return – perhaps a strand of your hair in exchange for a piece of bark, so the tree has a piece of you, and you have a piece of her.

- Back home, research your tree to find out what its wood has traditionally been used for in terms of tools, food, medicines, or other resources to cultivate a deeper sense of gratitude and connection. Find out whether your species of tree is under threat or is widespread? Is it native or invasive? Is there any interesting mythology linked to this type of tree?

- Return to your tree with a tape measure or ruler. Calculate the age of your tree. First measure the tree's girth with your tape measure (you can use your hand span to see how many it takes to fit round the tree at chest height, then measure your hand span with a ruler and multiply by the number of hands it took, e.g., 18cm hand span x 11 hands = 198cm girth). Although trees grow at varying rates, a trees girth will tend to grow at 2.5 cm each year, so divide the girth size in centimetres by 2.5 to work out its age. For example, 200cm girth divided by 2.5cm = 80 years old.

Note

Move from noticing trees to noting them. When you record trees by sketching, photographing, writing about or painting them, you attune yourself to their beauty in the moment. You also get to multiply the joy and engagement of that moment whenever you refer back to your "notes" or when you anticipate your next opportunity to creatively capture the beauty of trees.

#The100DayProject

The #100DayProject is a challenge aimed to encourage people to develop a creative habit (but there are many additional benefits) by committing to take small daily actions for 100 consecutive days. Apply it to your love of trees by choosing to record the beauty of a tree every day over a hundred days; immerse yourself in trees' beauty and follow your curiosity.

I undertook #The100DayProject in 2021, occasionally painting a small circular watercolour piece inspired by a tree I'd seen that day, but more often taking photographs (see the results on my @treeglee Instagram, #100DaysofTrees). I chose to link the tree and what it represented to an event or feeling from that day; in essence, to create a "tree-diary".

As a result of this immersive practice, I felt more attuned to trees' beauty and to my own thoughts, beliefs and responses – a greater sense of nature connectedness, self-connectedness and wellbeing. At the time I was experiencing negative side effects of menopause, and the focus helped me escape from my daily woes or put them in perspective, using trees as a conduit to navigate my way through whatever I was wrangling with.

Challenges like this or the Wildlife Trust's annual 30 Days Wild, have been shown to boost nature connectedness, wellbeing and conservation behaviours among participants. They can help you unwind at the end of a day and reflect on what went well or on what you've learned, or they can set you up creatively for the day ahead. If you use social media and embark on your own 100 day of trees project, please use the hashtags #100DaysofTrees #TreeGlee and #The100DayProject – this way all participants can share in each other's experiences, and embolden our connection and mutual wellbeing.

WAYS OF NOTICING AND NOTING THE BEAUTY OF TREES

TREE ART
This could be anything from detailed botanical illustrations, squiggly biro sketches, or simply capturing a moment of tree glee by creating a collage from leaves, bark and other tree materials you've collected. You could display collected materials each month or season. As my watercolour teacher @IrishHill suggests, "Focus on the feeling of the art rather than the aesthetics. Focus on breath and brush." This is a wonderful way to explore watercolour wellbeing: paint rough outlines of leaves as you inhale, and fill in with colour as you exhale.

TREE PHOTOGRAPHY
Rather than snapping away in haste, searching for the perfect shot, make this into a mindful and non-judgemental activity; anchor yourself with a few slow deep breaths, slow down to engage in the present moment, and focus your attention on what draws your curiosity. You will become consciously aware of the tiny details – perhaps the greenery, the leaves, the shape of the branches, the gnarly trunk. Limit yourself to taking six photographs. Let go of any judgement by carefully considering what's in the frame of the shot before you click. If judgemental thoughts pop up, observe, accept them, then let them pass. Replace judgement with curiosity and acceptance.

TREE *WABI-SABI*
This is the Japanese practice of finding beauty in imperfection, in nature; it's the acceptance and celebration of the "imperfect, impermanent and incomplete". It incorporates two pathways to nature connectedness – "Beauty" and "Compassion". Viewing the beauty of imperfect life is a helpful practice to our own wellbeing too, reminding us to let go of the pressures of perfection. Find a natural object that is perfectly imperfect yet brings you joy – a knobbly tree trunk or a ripped leaf. Then either photograph, sketch or paint it, celebrating its imperfection.

LEARN BONSAI

The ancient Japanese art of bonsai ("tray planting") involves growing small trees that mimic the shape of real-life trees. The main purposes of bonsai are for the grower to gain joy from their efforts and for the viewer to experience pleasure from contemplating the beauty of imperfection (symmetry is discouraged).

HONOUR A TREE

Write a tree or woodland tribute, poem, song, story or letter, or create a shrine to a tree with items that remind you of your favourite trees. You could visit the tree you've written about and create a simple ceremony giving thanks.

JOURNAL

The art of journaling is a useful wellbeing practice. It also brings your sensory experiences in nature alive by connecting to the language and visual imagination parts of your brain. There are no rules except to record your journal entries with date, time of day, season, weather conditions and a marker indicating which way north is (this helps connect you to a sense of place wherever you are in the natural world). Using words and/or pictures creatively, you could focus on *your* tree, the one you've befriended (see page 116), and maybe add a bark-rubbing or jot down three good things about being with trees (such as the sensations you feel, the wildlife you spot, the beauty, the impact of the weather or season). Analysis by the Nature Connectedness Research Group compared 50 members of the general population who noted down three good things in nature every day for five days with a control group of 42 people who noted three factual things, such as their meals. Two months after the exercise, the nature group demonstrated significantly increased nature connectedness and improvements in psychological health.[71]

Share

Share the observations you've made and the art you've created with others – curiosity is contagious, so you may well spark others' interest in trees. We explore the sharing of stories further in the chapter on listening, Chapter 7.

Another contagious source of joy, and one that is best shared with others, is play. Play grows the "Relationship" branch of wellbeing while also helping us learn quicker.

Play

Trees make perfect playmates. Remember how, as a child, trees conspired with you to keep you hidden? The seeker's head leaning against the tree, the hiders hiding behind their trunks or, if quick enough, up in their branches. Trees were your teammates, helping you avoid detection as you crept from tree to tree back to base.

You can gather acorns to make acorn people and conkers to battle with. You can make potions with leaves and berries, collect Pine cones and make fern pictures or crowns. And the fun you can have with leaves! I remember my dad brushing all the leaves from the garden into a huge pile at the foot of the slide into which we'd speed headfirst and again, on repeat.

Branches and twigs – limbs of trees delivered to our feet by wind and storm – can be anything! Our imagination can transform them into a broomstick, a microphone, a telescope or swords, spears and catapults. We can play "Pooh sticks" from bridges across streams, and make tiny tapestries on Y-shaped sticks. The possibilities are endless.

How about revisiting that time in our life when we saw trees as play partners and co-conspirators?

Prompt & Connect

The benefits of connecting and engaging with nature for awareness and mental health is undeniable. And a good way of ensuring this is part of your daily routine could be through a gentle nudge. A friend of mine, Karen Ward, runs a project called My Curious Eyes. Karen gives participants in her project a daily prompt for two weeks, such as "Texture", "Yellow", "Pattern".

They then go off and take photos that capture what the prompt made them curious about, and then share just one image each day. While the project is not specifically about nature, taking part in it ticks all three Notice, Note and Share boxes; and choosing trees as your subject matter to share will superboost your nature connectedness and all the positives that brings with it.

NINE TREE GAMES

CREATE A FOREST OBSTACLE COURSE

Use long logs to create balance beams and walkways, and short wide logs to hop from. Use twigs and branches found on the forest floor to mark out hopscotch and zigzag obstacles. Use short sticks to make arrows and crosses to indicate routes to take. Time each other to see who can make it round the fastest.

BUILD A BIRD HIDEOUT

Mark out a spot 2 or 3 metres away from the trees in the woodland or area of your garden that's most frequently visited by birds – this is where you will build your hideout. You'll need six or seven long thin sturdy branches or bamboo canes, some string, and plenty of leaves, ivy or evergreen tree cuttings for camouflage. Make a tepee by tying the long sticks together close to one end. With the tied end at the top and the sticks vertical, one by one pull the sticks outward to create a tepee shape, and push them into the ground to secure. To secure the tepee further, weave thin, flexible branches between the poles and cover the structure with the camouflage materials, leaving a peep hole to watch the birds from, using binoculars if you wish. If you can, leave the hideout up for a day or two before using it so the birds get used to it, then settle inside with a bird-spotting guide so you can identify birds correctly.

HOST AN AUTUMN TREE GAMES

Tap into the generosity of autumn with its conkers, Fir cones and falling leaves. Count who catches the most autumn leaves in five minutes. Hold leaf pile contests, seeing who can build the tallest pile of leaves before jumping into them. Throw leaves into the air at the end to celebrate the winner. Bake a freshly foraged apple and blackberry pie for the participants, and toast marshmallows round a fire at the end of the games.

FIND FACES ON TREE TRUNKS

Photograph them; give names to the faces; write stories about them.

GO ON A TREE-TREASURE HUNT

Make a list of woodland treasures to hunt for, such as Fir cones, feathers, Pine needles, a round(ish) leaf, a long thin leaf, a seed pod and a nut. Whoever is the first to collect all the items on the list wins. Turn your scavenger hunt into a challenge by timing it: 10 minutes to fill an empty matchbox with as many tree-related treasures as you can find with no duplicates.

PLAY A TREE MEMORY GAME

Place 15 tree items on a tray or clear space on the ground. Set a timer to one minute and let the participants concentrate on the collection before covering it up. Have someone remove one item from beneath the cover before exposing the collection once more. Whoever notices what the missing item is wins that go, replaces the item and then takes a turn to remove an item without anyone seeing. Repeat. You can move the items around to make it more difficult.

MAKE A POTION

Collect leaf litter, seed heads, berries, nuts and Pine needles in a cup or jug and add water and bicarbonate of soda. But don't drink it! We're just playing, remember.

SET A TREE POSE YOGA CHALLENGE

Bring one foot to rest just below or above your knee and balance on the other foot. Fix your gaze onto something in front of you to help you stay balanced. See who can remain in the tree pose the longest.

DOWNLOAD TREE TRUMPS®

Download this game from www.forestryengland.uk/resource/tree-trumps and challenge each other to find out which trees have the highest-ranking climb-ability, height and timber value.

Storytelling

"If you don't know the trees,
you may be lost in the forest;
but if you don't know
the stories, you may
be lost in life."

SIBERIAN ELDER

By noticing, then noting, the beauty of trees, we open a channel of reciprocity with them, receiving their gifts with thanks, grace and acknowledgement. In sharing what we've noticed and noted with others, we bring more people into this communion with trees, because when stories germinate, they can grow.

Storytelling bound ancient societies together, as well as providing crucial collective knowledge about where to find food and learn the landscape for survival. The men would go out tracking and hunting, while the women and children would harvest fruit and vegetables, pick berries, and gather bark from which to make cloth. Trees gave us the firelight by which to share stories, and round a fire the tribe would gather to exchange stories of the day.

The Story Circle

The story circle taps into our native "supernatural" ancestral roots and awakens our nervous system into remembering our innate connection with nature and with each other – our human need for community. So why not gather a group of friends round a fire and share stories of your nature connection experiences? You can use the following ideas to help the evening flow:

- Pass a talking stick to the storyteller.

Ask questions to garner stories from each other: find out which part of an experience in nature was the storyteller's favourite? What was the funniest, scariest, most surprising or educational moment?

- In your story, share details that bring to life all the sensory details you experienced – from the sound of the leaves to the surprise discoveries you found under deadwood or the wildlife you witnessed.

Cultural Connections

Our cultural connection with trees is mapped throughout our history. Trees are, in a way, our cultural comrades. By digging up our ancestral roots – discovering the stories that tell of tree traditions, celebrations and superstitions – we can find clues about why trees make us feel the way they do.

Trees were part of the fabric of our forebears' society; they influenced our cultural history, our behaviours, and became integral to our belief system. We believed specific trees and rituals offered the gift of fertility, enlightenment, good health or wisdom; for example, drinking from a stream into which hazelnuts drop brings wisdom, and passing through a cleft in an Ash tree cures sickness. And while science

and accumulation of knowledge has shifted our modern-day beliefs away from our pagan roots, our ancestral beliefs remind us that what mattered to us then – nurturing new life, protecting our families from harm and gaining wisdom with which to grow and develop – still matters to us today.

Trees make us feel good today because part of who we are is *because* of them.

But why should it matter to me that my Irish ancestors brought Hazel sticks into the home on May Day to ensure good health for the family, believing Hazel would offer protection? Turns out, it matters more than we might think, as connection to our past is good for us.

The past matters

The "Do You Know?" study, run by US psychologists Dr Marshall Duke and Dr Robyn Fivush, flagged up the importance of knowing our ancestral lineage and the stories that preceded ours. The study reported that the single best predictor of children's emotional health and happiness was "story". This is because the more a child knows of their family history and what they've been through in the past, the greater their self-esteem and the stronger their sense of control over their own life.[72]

Looking back gives us a sense of belonging. Genealogy depicts branches of generations, connected in a family tree and naturalists have long used tree diagrams to define different lineage of species. But trees offer more than a diagrammatic map to our past; trees take us back to where our own roots began. For trees, like stories themselves, are conduits of connection, they have routes as well as roots – routes to human past.

Making sense of life

Stories of The Tree of Life hark back to the very beginning, when the Earth flushed from brown to green. This tree shows up in folklore and mythology across the globe, from Ancient Egyptians, Vikings and Celts, to Romans, Hindus, Greek and Indigenous First Nations. In Celtic lore, the first man was created from an Alder and the first woman from a Rowan tree. Meanwhile, Greek mythology also saw us as descendants of the Rowan, which was created by Zeus. Whether the genesis stories told of humans descending from trees or that planting tree bark created the Earth itself, as with Canadian First Nation's Skywoman creation story, the tree is always present.

Cultural history points to a commonality: we all sought guidance from external sources, be it Gods, the Universe or tree spirits. This highlights an innate human need to work in connection with some "other". Tree stories offer numerous examples of that need for connection. In Norse mythology, the god Odin gains wisdom from the Ash tree known as Yggdrasil, whose roots and branches were believed to connect the nine worlds of the cosmos; in Indigenous stories of animism, sentience exists not just in humans but in animals, plants, rivers, rocks and mountains.

And the ancient Celtic belief that different trees served different mystical purposes perhaps enabled them to make better sense of life, to feel comforted and guided by the trees in their environment, to feel safe. Isn't that all any of us want?

Prophets and rituals

In ancient cultures, trees prophesized what the future might hold – who might we marry or whether the weather would be fair or stormy. The Maori have long listened to the whispers of the branches in the wind-omen tree of Ohoukaka Bay to determine if it is safe to go fishing. Indigenous people from North America and Canada gather round Cottonwood, Elm and Oak trees to hold council, gain guidance on when to plant corn and resolve conflicts. While divination rods made from Apple trees or Hazel helped guide people to water.

Trees were held up as sacred, so we worshipped them as idols. Believing they were endowed with spirits and bestowed with great powers, we'd celebrate Redwoods in America and Baobabs in Africa, and we'd dress them in ribbons. It was customary in some parts of Europe to burn a wooden effigy or small tree on a bride's wedding day, over which the bride would jump to summon the tree spirit to bless the bride with children.

In the UK, trees have been integral to our rituals. Our ancestors danced round still-rooted Birch maypoles for the Beltane festival, drank Druid Birch sap wine to celebrate Spring equinox and enjoyed the Celtic celebration of Samhain (now Halloween) using Birch twig bundles to drive out spirits to welcome in the new.

Protective allies

Protection is a common theme in tree mythology across multiple cultures. During the annual Hindu festival of Raksha Bandhan, people wrap trees in bright fabrics and colourful string to call upon a tree's power to protect their family.

The superstition of "knocking on wood" or saying "touch wood" is still widely used as an instinctive protective measure against something unwanted. It originated from the widespread belief about dryad and hamadryad spirits inhabiting trees; ancient priests would knock on a tree to summon the tree spirits to help ward off evil spirits and offer protection.

Specific trees were also deemed sacred protectors, and none more so than the sacred Rowan tree. Norse mythology tells of the Rowan tree bending over a fast-flowing river to save Thor, God of Thunder, from being swept away into the Underworld. The Celts carved walking sticks from Rowan, carried Rowan bark or protective crosses tied with red thread from Rowan wood in their pockets, fastened Rowan sprigs to cattle, and planted Rowan trees beside homes to ward off malevolent faeries. In Medieval Britain the sacred Rowan was thought to protect against witchcraft and enchantment because the five-pointed-star pentagram, an ancient symbol of protection, is embedded in the bottom of every Rowan berry, opposite its stalk. To this day, Rowan trees can be found with remarkable regularity lining concrete streets and planted in front gardens, such is their cultural significance.

Similarly, we can still find evidence in our homes of the long-held belief in the Oak tree and its acorns as protectors, be it in the acorn toggle at the end of the string of a window blind or as carvings topping the newel posts of stairs. While outside in the streets, Oaks still stand vigil over villages.

In stories old and new, trees have foretold the future and protected our present. Even the wand used by the fictitious Harry Potter to fight his nemesis, the dark lord, Voldemort, is made of Holly – another tree associated with protection.

Digging Up Our Roots

I invite you to gather stories about trees – stories about your own experiences, stories you've learned about the myths and legends of trees in your own culture, and real stories of remarkable trees that offer insight into life from a tree's perspective. Then share these stories far and wide. Let's tell of trees.

I'll start ... did you know that folklore tells how catching an Oak leaf before it touches the ground means you'll have good health during the cold winter? Or that acorns were believed to keep illness at bay and protect against lightning strikes, so carrying them in pockets became a common tradition to give the carrier longevity of life?

Fantastic facts

If you're more interested in facts than folklore, you might choose to learn more about dendrochronology, which tells us the age of trees based on the number of rings inside their trunk and captures their own embodied history about which years saw good growth and which were leaner.

Or perhaps the histories of amazing trees cultivate your curiosity the most. If so, why not explore the stories of the oldest recorded tree (a 4,854-year-old Great Basin Bristlecone Pine called Methuselah who germinated around 2,832 years BCE) or the only slightly younger 4,000-year-old Llangernyw Yew who occupies a tiny churchyard in North Wales? These trees seeded in ancient times, when people lived in roundhouses and the global population was between a mere 27 and 50 million.

In the US, since 1940, the American Forests National Big Tree Program has kept a national register of champion trees, with over 750 on its database.

A champion tree is a superstar of its species, the largest of its kind. For example, 2,000-year-old General Sherman in Sequoia National Park is the largest living organism on Earth – 275 feet tall, a 36-foot diameter trunk at its base (as wide as three car lanes), and a total volume of over 52,000 cubic feet. The program awards points for each measure, so the tree needs strong scores across the combined three measurements (height, width and volume) to secure champion status. For example, Hyperion, the tallest tree in the world at over 379 feet high, isn't a champion tree because its 15-foot diameter trunk doesn't compare to fellow Coast Redwood (Sequoia sempervirens), the Lost Monarch, who at 321 feet has a 26-foot diameter trunk.

Alternatively, your interest might be piqued by the 40,000 strong Pando Aspen colony in Fishlake National Forest, Utah, USA, which spreads out across

106 acres, growing from a single set of roots. Then coming back to Hyperion; this neck-craning Coast Redwood lives on a hillside from which 96 per cent of his family and neighbouring old growth community have sadly been logged for timber. Cautionary tree tales like this are aplenty.

If trees could talk

Then there are the tales of trees who witnessed pivotal moments in history. Like the Tree of Hippocrates, who, if he could talk, would tell the story of the Father of Medicine and how he provided shade for Hippocrates and his students during many an insightful lesson.

The Bodhi Fig tree (known as the "tree of awakening") might whisper about how it was beneath the shade of her own heart-shaped leaves where the spiritual teacher Siddhartha Gautama, who became the Buddha himself, achieved enlightenment following seven weeks (49 days) of meditation without moving from that shaded spot around 500 years BCE.

Or 4,000 miles away on the bank of the River Thames, the ancient 2,500-year-old Ankerwycke Yew would blush as she spouted about the trysts of King Henry VIII and his soon-to-be second wife, Anne Boleyn, who courted beneath her bows in the 1530s. Then she'd reveal how, hundreds of years earlier, in 1215, the *Magna Carta* – one of history's most influential and important constitutional documents – was signed by King John under her very boughs.

Story-sharing

Trees stand as a record of and tribute to the past, and a reminder to inspire action to co-write our combined future. Yet trees do not have a voice with which to share these stories – that is up to us. I invite you to read and share these stories and many more in my own collection of tree tales which you can find over at www.TreeGlee.co.uk.

What's Your Treestory?

"A tree is a little bit
of the future."

FRANCK PRÉVOT,
WANGARI MAATHAI

The life choices we make are like branches, forking to the left or right, depending on the decisions we make and the directions we take. At a tree's centre is its core, the heartwood, the central supporting pillar. As long as the outer layers of heartwood remain intact, the tree will never lose strength or decay. Similarly, the layers of our own lives make us who we are. We are the sum total of all our experiences – joyful and painful.

It can be cathartic to look back over our life; to gather the lessons learned and reflect on the triumphs or tragedies. Our life story is unique to us. Yet, if we gather snapshots from our life – an early birthday party, a first kiss, a teenage friendship, a first home, a wedding day, a birth and other milestone events, it is likely that trees will appear on at least some of those images. Our histories have trees planted throughout.

Trees provide a kind of comforting arboreal "soundtrack" to our lives, always there during times of great delight and times of dire need. They were there at the very beginning of our human story and are co-stars in our individual life stories too. And those entwined trees can act as memory keepers, like a memory stick, holding the years of our lives on it.

Bearing Fruit

For some, trees are woven into their own life story purposefully, with devotion. This is the case for Hussam Saraf, who recently claimed the world record for the most types of fruit on a single tree (his tree bears 10 different fruits across five species) from his leafy, suburban home in Shepparton, Victoria, Australia.

Hussam's treestory began with Fig trees in his birthplace of Iraq. Fig trees were used to teach Hussam and his classmates the horticultural technique of singular grafting. During his school holidays at his grandparent's farm, Hussam's passion for gardening grew, his knowledge expanding from Fig to Date, Citrus and Pomegranate trees. He carried this knowledge with him when he moved from Iraq to Australia in 2009.

Hussam's record-breaking Peach, Plum, Apricot, Cherry and Almond tree is the result of a decade of devotion. He started with a Nectarine tree seedling, and gradually grafted branches of other trees onto it. Each grafted branch is a unique tree in itself, united through the grafting process to create a single multi-fruit tree offering a variety of fruits.

With fruit and wonder in such abundance, Hussam invites friends and relatives to taste it, gives spare fruit to his neighbours, and has even opened his tropical garden, rich in Banana, Coconut, Kumquat and Rosella trees, to the public to share the fruits of his labour further. As Hussam says, "It's not just a garden, it's a community."

That unity is what gives Hussam's treestory meaning, for his multi-fruit tree is aligned with his work as a multicultural officer at the local public school. He sees the tree as his multicultural community's tree – diverse fruits unite on the tree, just as diverse traditions, races and religions come together in his community. Hussam humbly tells us, "My multicultural work and gardening work I see as one, I'm grafting it all together."

This record-breaking tree provides a meaningful message about what Hussam calls "peaceful coexistence", but also offers another important message – that of aiming high, putting in the hard graft (excuse the pun), setting a goal and trying your best to achieve it.

And Hussam's treestory isn't over yet. His next goal is to achieve the world record for the largest gardening lesson, which currently stands at 280 people – he's aiming to teach a thousand!

Creating Your Own Treestory

Even if we've never worked with trees or tended them, trees can still have great meaning. City-dwellers, rural villagers and suburbanites alike will recall trees in their lives if given the catalyst to remember. Story-telling can be that impetus for remembering. We can map out our lives in trees and use trees as markers of chapters in our life as we ponder on what we did and what we learned during those parts of our life's narrative. We can research the symbolism of specific trees we've shared our lives with to uncover potential synergies between the trees' meanings and our life events. Just as Hussam grafted multiple fruit trees together, we can graft the trees we've encountered throughout our lives together into one unique treestory.

My treestory

Once upon a time, there was a writer who loved trees. She wasn't a botanist or a forester, nor a gardener or silviculturist (one who cares for and cultivates woodland), just a woman, once a girl, who adored trees.

As she enters the next chapter of her life, she reflects on what she did before, and she remembers.

Her memories dance around the Apple tree in the back garden of her childhood bungalow in Fair Oak village. When she closes her eyes, she can just about recall the first few steps of the climb, which branches and footholds she held and stood on to reach her "treehouse".

Her mind rests on an all-time favourite memory of her 10-year-old self, stretching out on a blue floral 1970s' sun-lounger under the deep shade of a delightful Catawba (Indian Bean) tree, reading *Charlie and the Chocolate Factory* as dappled sunlight shines through its giant lime-coloured leaves, the air bathed in gold.

Her mum sits upright besider her in an orange sun-lounger, the kind with white plastic arms that send the back of the chair downward and lift your feet up when you pull them. Her mum smiles into the sunshine, eyes closed. Happy.

Seven-and-a-half years later the girl (now almost a woman) is standing on the lower gun deck of Nelson's flagship, *HMS Victory* in Portsmouth dry dock. A ceilidh is being held in memory of her mother, Denise. All she can see is the wood – so much timber – as she looks around her at the ornate windows, heavy guns, yellow lanterns and white gold-lined walls. Later, she learns it took 6,000 trees from 100 acres of woodland to build this 226-foot-long ship that fought in the Battle of Trafalgar. She's not sure what her mother would've

made of people dancing in her honour onboard, and she'll never know.

Her mind races forward to when she became a parent herself and she stands at the entrance of a field in Hursley village and looks toward her "Wishing Tree" and makes a wish. That transports her to the memory of another special tree, which she named the "Love Tree", a tall slender Yew tree in the woodland of a leafy suburb she once called home.

Later, while researching this very book, she discovers the English Yew is one of just three native conifers to the British Isles; and they were so prolific in her home county of Hampshire, they were called the Hampshire Weed. Her "Love tree" is no such thing!

Snowing now, the soft white flakes rest gently on the Yew's branches, a tiny bird lands overhead and snowflakes fall from the strong-scented needles. "Oh, Miss Yew I miss you!" she says.

Evergreen adventures assemble as she's whisked off to marvel at the magnificent tall Cedar trees and mossy green floor in Emerald Forest, Whistler, Canada, where she stands, enchanted, next to her friend and guide, Tanis.

And she's back in Canada again, picking a red, yellow and green leaf that matches her hat from the forest floor and smiling widely for a photo. She's walking with a group of women through the rainforest of British Columbia. She holds on to a crooked Arbutus tree, a piece of its cinnamon-red bark peeling off in her hand, as they climb higher. She's then blown away by what she sees before her – a huge sculpture of an ancient mastodon, built from driftwood in a location kept secret. She feels the joy of the discovery of such a remarkable treasure, and marvels at how each driftwood piece has been carried here by its creator and assembled close to the clouds. The camaraderie of the wonderful women she's sharing this with fills her heart.

Soon she's walking around a labyrinth on a retreat on Bowen Island, Vancouver, before standing with her friend Debra, their hands on their hearts. They sigh deeply in awe of Opa, the 1,000-year-old Douglas Fir in Squamish territory, its base peppered with offerings of sage and sweetgrass. She wraps her arms round this beautiful tree, its bark wet yet welcoming. Opa is marked by axe strikes and scarred by saws, but is one of just two trees which avoided the clear-cutting on the island in the early part of the century. Opa is a survivor.

Her past fades into her present and she turns to the page of her current chapter.

My tree-present

My treestory – a recollection of trees that have woven their way into my life – is not over yet. My life continues to be filled with trees.

Huge Horse Chestnuts hug my home and offer up a year-long bounty: in autumn, the spiky cases of their mahogany conkers fall to the ground.; in spring, a bewildering chaos of white-pink blossom attracts bees; in summer, palmate-toothed leaves stretch out, like hands, to greet me with layered shades of green; and in winter, their bare branches remind me to rest.

In nearby parkland, I delight in the evergreen Holme Oak that grows between two Sycamore trees and the ancient Horse Chestnut at the far end of the field. These are the trees I visit if I need to get away, to have a think. They shelter me from the world and soothe occasional tears, giving me permission to be human as I confide in them.

Then there's the 250-year-old Great British Oak tree I'm now guardian of, who was alive at the start of the Industrial Revolution. I've named her the Magic Faraway Tree, because (as in the famous Enid Blyton story of the same name) Oaks support more wildlife than any other tree and there are animal-home shaped holes at the base of her trunk. I also affectionately call this tree Oma (grandmother), in honour of the almighty Opa (grandfather) I hugged in British Columbia. And, like all kindly grandmothers, she lets me sit on her lap as her lower trunk has bent to provide a seat from where I can look up and out at her leafy branches.

I love that we now have a Catawba (Indian Bean) tree in the front garden

of our home. And, while it may be more sparse-leafed than the one from my childhood, the colours of the leaves still pop against a blue summer sky.

Just as hearing a song or smelling a scent can spark a strong memory, so too can seeing a tree – like the two Acers my mother-in-law gave me for my 40th birthday, which I can take with me wherever I go and grow, and which remind me of the sprawling red Acer my dad planted beneath my bedroom window.

I was raised with long suburban gardens, woodland dens and climbing trees. Now, nearing 50, I am supported by woodland walks and tending to trees of my own. They're part of me, part of my life, part of my story.

Treestory Glee

Treestories can help us feel good through the memories they muster, the kinship they spark and the joy they rekindle.

Hussam's treestory tended to every single PERMA-V branch of wellbeing (see Chapter 4). Doing what he loved gave him Positive Emotion and was Engaging. Sharing his work with his local community helped him cultivate his Relationships. Working on this project was purposeful and gave life Meaning, while reaching his goal and breaking the world record gave him a great sense of Accomplishment. Gardening, being a labour-intensive outdoor pursuit, grew his Vitality branch. A veritable feel-good treestory in all the ways.

For me, each tree in my life has made me feel better – my childhood trees offered adventure, comfort and shade, they made me feel happy, safe and home. Magnolias, Acers and Cherry trees always make me feel warm, joyful, satisfied. Those big Canadian grandparent trees made me feel awe and wonder and hope, and the trees that surround my home now make me feel reassured, held and inspired.

The joy of story is the capacity and possibility to write a happy ending with green ink, one in which all living things who share this planet can flourish together. We hold the pen – what we write next is up to us.

WHAT'S YOUR ———————————
TREESTORY?

- Ask yourself who are the arboreal heroes of your life story? Which rooted marvels have been there rooting for you? If you don't know what species they were, can you discover this through photographs or a visit? If not, why not make up a name for them instead? Like my "love tree".

- Find out more about these trees' stories. For example, the Indian Bean tree which means so much to me (see my treestory on page 140) refers to the local Native American tribe near to where the tree was first recorded by a Mr Catesby. His transcription of their name, Catawba, was incorrectly recorded as Catalpa, hence the tree now being known as the Southern Catalpa. To honour the native name, I shall always refer to it as Catawba. How much richer our connections with trees can be when we know their own stories.

- What do those species of trees symbolize? Use Google to see what you can uncover. Are there any interesting synergies between their symbolic meaning and what was happening in your life when they became important to you?

- How have the specific trees in your own treestory made you feel throughout your life? Which ones restored you and made you feel grounded? Which trees reassured you and made you feel comforted and safe? Which ones revitalized you and made you feel happy and alive? Which trees have reconnected you to the present, to people, to home? And which trees have garnered your respect and made you feel small and humble in their presence?

- Break your treestory up into a timeline of trees: childhood, adolescence, twenties, thirties and so on. Write a few lines in a journal about what each of your timeline trees has taught you so far? What did you achieve during those years? What challenges or obstacles did you overcome? How did you deal with the transitions between trees? How might you use these observations and integrate these lessons in writing your best next chapter?

- Look back at the seasons of your year so far. What fruits of wisdom did you gather during the autumn harvest? What could you celebrate about your spring? You might wish to save this exercise for a pre-New-Year reflection.

- Create a treestory vision board for the year ahead. Write down or cut images or words from a magazine and stick them onto your vision board to represent your hopes, aspirations and goals for the year ahead.
- Who were the key characters in the chapters of your treestory? Which childhood friends did you climb trees and visit the woods with? Could you reconnect with them and visit those trees? Who has most recently entered your life and do you have any tree connections? There may be people with whom you connected with as a direct result of your shared tree enthusiasm.
- Consider going on a treestory pilgrimage to revisit the trees from your past chapters, but only if it feels like the right thing to do. Housing estates were built on my childhood woods and Google Earth suggests my beloved Apple tree may no longer be there, which would be sad to see, so I prefer to hold her in the magical place in my memory.
- Show gratitude, admiration and respect to your trees in the form of a poem, a song, a diary entry or a letter.
- Find your tree-twin. For a bit of fun and connection, consider this: if you were a tree, which tree would you be? What is your essence? Write down words that capture who you are now, who you've been and who you aspire to be. What are your character strengths? Connecting our sense of self to a particular tree can help us feel a deeper kinship with one. Might you be a tree that features in your treestory? For example, might I be an Alder, like those growing in my woodland, which represent strength in adversity (hence why Venice is built entirely on Alder wood as it gets stronger when submerged in water); or perhaps I'd be a Beech tree because of my love for books?

PART THREE

RECIPROCATION

A Harmonious Approach to Tree Care

"The best time to plant a tree was 20 years ago. The second best time is now."

CHINESE PROVERB

Today, trees are in trouble. But you know that already. You've seen the forests on fire, the logging trucks queuing to take the last few per cent of old grandmother-tree logs, having already taken the other 97 per cent; you've seen the increasingly frequent flooding caused by soil erosion and reduced water absorption (a knock-on effect of logging).

Since mankind first began felling them, we've lost almost half (46 per cent) of all trees on Earth, and we're on a fast track to lose 50 per cent of what's left over the coming century. As I type this sentence, another seven acres has been lost – two trees per person per year, which adds up to more than 15 billion trees annually, between birthdays.

Despite the promises and the urgency of reducing deforestation, which, along with burning fossil fuels, is a main cause of global warming, satellite images reveal that 2020 to 2021 saw the highest level of deforestation of the Amazon rainforest in over 15 years!

Then there's the gradual extinction of 70 per cent of the world's land species who live in forests, the potential loss of life-saving drug treatments that are yet to be discovered, and the ever-rising populace of 80 million people per year versus the ever-decreasing access to Mother Earth's finite resources.

Even though scientists race to fill back-up seed banks in order to be able to replant the one in five tree species at risk of extinction, many trees can't be preserved like this.

Helping Trees Helps Us

Considering all they do for us (see Chapter 1), don't we owe trees a bit of reassurance? Trees have been looking after us our whole lives, perpetually giving while we took the gifts from their outstretched limbs and ran away. Yet, in a game of people versus planet where the score is 1–0, we lose when we win.

Tending to trees is a win-win for *all* life. And the principal pathway to wellbeing is a healthy planet. Scientists know this; Indigenous people know this; and, in all honesty, we know this too. But what motivates us to act on this knowledge?

If our own self-destruction won't motivate us to act, what *will* persuade us to change our deep-rooted behaviours and help reverse the damage we're doing to the natural world?

According to Daniel H Pink in his book, *Drive: The Surprising Truth About What Motivates Us*, the carrot and stick approach of rewarding good behaviour and punishing bad behaviour is no longer effective in an increasingly disengaged world, where we have swapped curiosity for compliance and where there is less empathy and more apathy.[73]

Motivation and engagement are complex topics, but Pink's conclusions are worth noting: it is *purpose* that seems to motivate action the most.

Of course, a purpose that engages one person may not engage another. For some, there is no purpose greater than saving the planet, and ergo ourselves. For others, perhaps, saving the Earth may feel too big a purpose to engage in amid an already-full daily timetable of tasks. How do we fit "saving the rainforests" into our never-ending to-do lists?

A Balanced Approach

What if we made the purpose more manageable, doable, bite-sized? An elephant, as the analogy goes, is easy to eat one bite at a time. Yes, big ideas, big voices and a sense of urgency are still desperately needed to prevent ecosystem collapse and save our good green world, but trying to tip the balance in favour of all living things is a step in the right direction and a less daunting approach. Finding balance might feel more achievable and less overwhelming as a purpose than saving the entire planet.

And perhaps a balanced approach – rather than all-or-nothing – might more readily galvanize the masses? Because it's critical that we all do something!

I say balanced harmony is a good place to start.

The Haudenosaunee Confederacy (also known as the Iroquois Confederacy and the League of Five Nations), the first, oldest and longest-lasting participatory democracy on Earth, is rooted in harmony. They have a unique constitution in which nature, society and law are equal partners, playing proportionately important roles in balanced harmony with each other.

If the rest of the world adopted a less egocentric and more "eco-centric" approach, such as this, we could create balance between:

1. give and take
2. tree-care and self-care
3. tree protection and plantation
4. ecology and economy
5. consumption and reduction.

So, let's explore this balanced approach to action.

Balancing give & take

Our ancestors harvested trees for firewood and shelter, but were selective, taking only what they needed, and left the forest to regenerate.

Various Indigenous cultures, particularly those in North America and Canada, partook in what's known as the "honourable harvest", respecting the personhood of the tree. Before the harvest, rather than taking without asking first, they requested permission from the tree. They would never fell a tree housing a nest, and never take more than half of a crop or wooded area. During the harvest they'd protect neighbouring trees to minimize damage, and after the harvest they'd leave a token of gratitude behind, such as tobacco, a lock of hair or, in Maori tradition, a hand-carved sculpture.

They'd honour a felled tree further by ensuring every piece was used, nothing wasted and something beautiful crafted.

What if we used balanced give and take as our compass of care? Each time we think we need a new bag or top, we might ask, "What would the balanced approach be?" The answer might be to make or make-do, or to buy a T-shirt from a company that uses organic, fair-trade cotton and plants a tree with each purchase. When we're thinking about where to go on holiday, considering balance in our decision-making might navigate us toward an eco-tourism holiday which gives deforesters an alternative income to chopping down trees, or a staycation at a permaculture farm where we can learn how to grow our own food.

Balancing tree-care & self-care

Just as trees make us feel better in the ways we've explored throughout this book, taking care of trees makes us feel better too. In fact, tree-care action grows every one of the PERMA-V branches of wellbeing (see Chapter 4). Tackling tasks together and working toward shared goals in a group unites people for a common purpose. This type of action facilitates social connections, growing the Meaning (M) and Relationships (R) branches. Achieving those goals offers a sense of mastery and Accomplishment (A). The task (conservation work, for example) might simultaneously enable flow and work up a sweat, growing the Engagement (E) and Vitality (V) branches too. What's more, doing something good to benefit the planet provides one of the greatest and most gleeful feelings of all, known as "giver's glow", growing the Positive Emotion (P) branch extensively.

Turns out, giving back to these gentle giants through action has the power to make us feel better than any other activity, especially when we strive for balanced harmony for the benefit of all.

Balancing tree protection & plantation

From Indigenous people to scientists, botanists and ecologists, those remarkable humans who've devoted their lives to trees or retained a strong kinship with them know reciprocal action for trees must be balanced between protecting them and planting them.

Ancient woodland and trees that have persisted for centuries are irreplaceable. It takes decades, even centuries, for trees to grow into mature forests. And when trees are destroyed or degraded, carbon is released back into the atmosphere. Indeed, existing old forests are better carbon sinks and more resilient to fires, storms and droughts than their younger counterparts. So, while it is vital that we plant more trees, forest plantation doesn't always compensate for forest destruction, i.e., it's not enough just to plant trees. We need to protect them too.

Meg Lowman, author of *The Arbornaut*, told me, "There are very few situations where a creative solution can't allow a big tree to stay in place. Roads can be curved and shopping malls can have courtyards rather than cutting down big trees and planting tiny ones that will take decades and centuries to achieve their mature canopy status.

"Planting trees is always important, but it's a big lottery if those trees will ever recover all the amazing biodiversity that originally lived in the forest before it was cut down. The best and easiest thing to do is to *save* big mature trees. They don't need daily watering or as much protection from being eaten or knocked down and they capture the most carbon."

The Woodland Trust echoes this priority for protection: "We desperately need to protect the few Ancient Woodlands we have left. When allowed to flourish, they can help mitigate some of the environmental consequences of industry and society in ways that a younger forest cannot always match."

Turn to page 168 to find practical ways you can help balance tree protection and plantation.

Balancing ecology & economy

Unfortunately, some current food systems destroy ecosystems. Methane from farmed livestock is a greenhouse gas, while making room to grow agricultural crops is a main reason behind deforestation. Both contribute to the climate crisis, and the latter creates a false economy as it reduces land quality and productivity long-term.

Clear-cutting is another problem. On the Southern Coast of British Columbia, 3.3 million hectares of old growth 2,000 year-old Cedar and Fir forests once stood. Today 860,000 hectares remain, with only 260,000 of those protected. Logging here contributes to approximately 64 million tonnes of carbon emissions a year.

In 2010 the Zero Net Deforestation Act bill was passed, which requires an equal size area of any deforested area be planted. However, without old growth Mother Trees, which have the most robust mycorrhizal networks, the chances for any newly-planted seedlings to survive is far less. In addition to ripping soil societies apart, overt clear-cutting is now thought to trigger landslides and flooding.

Yet, with many local people relying on logging for income and the amount of harvestable wood lessening, the forestry industry must become sustainable in order to survive.

And a two-year Ancient Forest Alliance study released in 2021 concludes that society is better off when old growth forests are protected rather than logged. The report reveals the greater regional economic benefit that Southern Vancouver Island old growth forests could contribute through tourism and salmon habitat protection rather than harvesting ancient forest timber.[74]

While old growth logging is being deferred in some places until sustainable solutions can be found, it seems that government intervention is required. To balance the needs of people and planet, funding could provide retraining and financial support for loggers and First Nations who stand to lose revenue and jobs as forestry policies change. Such efforts could bridge the gap to enable the transition from old growth to second growth logging, the processing of planted sustainable forests and new economic

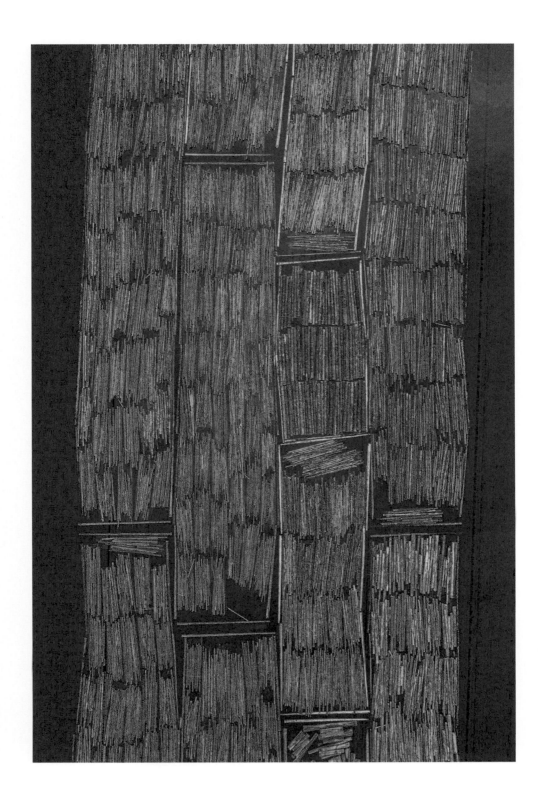

opportunities for local people via tourism, for example.

Fortunately, there are many initiatives and possibilities that offer glimmers of hope in addressing these problems – like *komorebi* shards of sunlight shining through the trees in a darkened forest – as we will discover in Chapter 10.

Balancing consumption & reduction

It's clear we need to find balance in a world of finite resources where consumption is ever-growing.

The "hedonic treadmill" describes the perpetual loop of achieving or buying more and experiencing immediate pleasure, which soon fades causing us to desire more; and on and on it goes, because we'll always need another shot.

According to the economic "law of diminishing marginal utility", devised by Prussian economist Hermann Heinrich Gossen in 1854, the more we have of something, the less happiness we gain from it. This, combined with our adaptation to material gains, explains why the next toy, pair of shoes, achievement or promotion doesn't boost our happiness for long.

Enough (literally) is enough. Our consumer choices make a difference. Where we shop, what we buy and how we recycle, reuse and reduce what we buy affects the health of our planet both now and in the future. There are a multitude of things you can act on today, tomorrow and forever, as shown in the Responsible Consumer Goals action list on pages 160–61. Take a look at this before making your shopping list and, before long, these actions will become habitual and you'll have saved many trees. By making small changes, together we can make a big impact.

Rekindle Harmony

Through devotional care and making good choices we can rekindle that harmonious and balanced relationship we once had with trees. As we will see in the next chapter, whether those choices lead to big or small actions, all play a role in creating balanced harmony. And it's our responsibility.

RESPONSIBLE
CONSUMER GOALS

WHERE?

- Shop locally and seasonally for groceries to minimize your carbon footprint, reducing how far your food has to travel. Avoid food with plastic packaging too.
- When shopping online, use the Ecosia search engine, which invests 80 per cent of its profits to plant trees.
- Shop from environmentally friendly brands with clear policies and buy Fair Trade or Rainforest Alliance products to ensure everyone along the supply chain is treated fairly; the Rainforest Alliance's goal is that "people and nature thrive in harmony".
- Buy from companies which plant a tree in exchange for your custom.

WHAT?

- Reduce or stop buying red meat (especially beef) and dairy. Eighty per cent of deforestation is caused by clearing for grazing and feeding livestock. Cows and sheep are also responsible for much methane (one of the greenhouse gases). Join the Meatless Monday movement, then gradually eat more plant-based foods and consider going vegetarian or vegan.
- Avoid buying products containing palm oil; read the ingredients labels to check. Approximately 27 million hectares of land has been deforested to produce palm oil, which is often found in chocolate, ice cream, baked goods, bread, noodles, soap, detergent, shampoo and make-up. As consumers we are partially responsible for the loss of the Amazon when we buy products created from clear-cutting, so also avoid buying soy and unsustainable coffee, which are farmed in similar ways.
- Know where your timber originates from. Most UK wood is grown sustainably. Buy wood products and furniture that is Forest Stewardship Council (FSC) certified, which proves the wood was legally felled.
- Buy products from recycled materials or buy second-hand.
- Try tree-free alternatives to paper and wood, such as bamboo, which is sustainable as bamboo stalks grow back immediately after harvesting.

HOW?

- Avoid single-use items. Disposable paper, cardboard and wooden products are better for the environment than plastic, but reusable materials are even better to minimize waste. Consider washable cloth napkins, dishcloths, handkerchiefs, nappies and period pants. Use reusable containers rather than paper or plastic lunch bags; carry with you a reusable coffee cup, water bottle and shopping bags.
- Reuse seeds. After eating fruit, dry the seeds, pop them into a bag and distribute them on your walks. Let nature germinate them.
- Go as paperless as possible to save 24 square feet of forest – the average household saving after one year of paperless billing. Choose paperless billing with your bank and your utility providers. Unsubscribe from paper magazines and newspapers. Opt-out of junk mail – over 100 million trees are used to produce the junk mail sent to US mailboxes each year. Refuse receipts.
- Recycle newspapers. Doing so saves 250 million trees a year!
- Use both sides of printer paper and only print when necessary. Buy recycled or hemp printer paper. Look for "post-consumer" recycled fibre where possible.
- Reuse wrapping paper and delivery packaging. According to Greenpeace, 3kg of CO_2 emissions come from manufacturing 1kg of wrapping paper.
- Use your phone to take notes instead of paper.
- Use recycled toilet paper.
- Make your own cards from recycled card or send digital e-cards. In the UK alone, at least 150 million cards are delivered by Royal Mail each Christmas, which equates to approximately 50,000 trees.
- Use second-hand boxes, suitcases and storage boxes when moving house.
- Choose a living Christmas tree with its root ball attached. To enhance its chance of survival, bring it inside for no more than 10 days and keep it in an outbuilding for a day or so before and afterwards to acclimatize it. If choosing an artificial tree, keep it for one or two decades to justify its carbon footprint. Otherwise, choose a real tree from a local farm where land is saved from alternative development and trees provide habitats for wildlife. Be sure to recycle the tree afterwards by using it as garden fertilizer or using a collection and recycling service.

What We Can Do to Reciprocate

"UNLESS someone like you cares a whole awful lot, nothing is going to get better. It's not."

DR SEUSS, *THE LORAX*

Giving back to the trees is not just about planting trees for the good of the planet; it's about planting a partnership and developing a relationship with them. It's about tending to them and speaking up for them, so we may save the trees already in the ground. It's about educating ourselves about worthwhile initiatives and cultivating responsible consumer habits that help rather than harm forests. This chapter outlines the practical reciprocal actions that make a real difference.

Tree Protection

Recent figures reveal only 7 per cent of native ancient woodland in the UK is thriving, while logging practices worldwide are also proving unsustainable, so protecting the trees and forests we already have is critical. Whether that protection comes by developing *around* trees, conserving ancient woodlands or managing forests sustainably, the message from conservationists and climate-change scientists is clear: Plant trees please, but prioritize saving those we already have.

HOW TO PROTECT ──────────
OUR TREES

- Become a tree warden to protect local trees or join a deforestation watch group to monitor local lumber companies.
- Read about forest defenders and find inspiration to protect your local woodland.
- Research and record your local tree heritage, add to ancient tree inventories (see Useful Resources, page 184) and map old woods and trees to help protect them.
- Donate to tree-conservation charities and encourage the companies you work for and deep-pocketed philanthropists to do the same. These could include Greenpeace, Rainforest Action Network, The Nature Conservancy, The Mother Tree Project and International Tree Foundation.
- Balance conservation donations by donating to reforestation projects, such as Plant a Tree Today Foundation (pattfoundation.org) or One Tree Planted.

See more ways to protect trees on page 165, opposite.

People Power

Over a decade ago, the UK's Environment Secretary was forced to make a U-turn on the consultation into the sale of between 150,000 and 258,000 hectares of the country's forestry estate, when a public petition received over half a million signatures. A victory for the collectivism of people power, trees and the planet.

But tree protection can start on a smaller scale. When I worked briefly for her publishing company, The Body Shop founder Dame Anita Roddick told me, "If you think you're too small to have an impact, try going to bed with a mosquito." Indeed, in Sheffield (UK) in 2018, the passionate protest of 83-year-old campaigner Roy Millington galvanized locals into taking a stand, and 20 healthy trees on one road were saved. The planned removal of the trees was part of a long-term council initiative to improve roads, which had already overseen the loss of thousands of mostly healthy street trees.

The trees Roy set out to protect were planted in 1919 as living war memorials to honour 401 local lads, 61 of whom were killed during the First World War. So, Roy sat on the steps of the local Town Hall for up to 10 hours a week holding a placard. The "Western Road

Remembers" campaign grew over the months that followed, and the protest worked.

Similarly engaged citizens are tipping the balance in the planet's favour by marching in protest, spreading awareness and shouting from the rooftops about what needs to happen to address the challenges of climate change. You can too!

- Become an ambassador for your local trees.
- Write letters and attend meetings with council decision makers, insurers and city planners. Find and quote national planning policy about ancient woodland protection and show reports and statistics about the lack of urban tree-felling justification in response to unwarranted subsidence claims.[75] Ensure your local authority has ordinances to prevent local trees from being felled.
- Start or join a peaceful protest to defend endangered sites and species and raise awareness about the plight of trees.
- Start and sign petitions to stop clear-cutting, protect ancient woodland and save street trees. Share them on social media to encourage others to sign too.

TREE MAMA

Sometimes, when one person takes a stand for trees, this can evolve into a whole conservation movement, as is true for Kenyan Wangari Maathai (1940–2011), aka Mama Miti, "the mother of trees".

Over her lifetime, Wangari stood up for women's rights, bravely spoke up about political corruption and, as founder of the Green Belt Movement, was responsible for the planting of 30 million trees and the conservation of many more, while simultaneously empowering women to unite for social reform. In turn, she became the first African woman to win the Nobel Peace Prize (for environmental and humanitarian efforts).

As a child, Wangari had watched tree after tree fall as British colonialists cut them down to create space for tea plantations. Radically, her mother decided to send her to school, rare for girls at that time; and Wangari went on to study in the USA. Back home in post-colonial Kenya, the well-educated Wangari noticed how broken both the economy and the ecology of her nation were. Her countryfolk still needed to fell trees to plant and export tea, tobacco and coffee, long after the British left in 1963.

In 1977, Wangari travelled from village to village, persuading people, especially women, to start tree nurseries and plant trees as part of the Green Belt Movement. Saplings from those nurseries were offered as tribal peace tokens when the President tried to stir up trouble for her. She protested against the President's deforestation plans and, despite imprisonment, persisted to make her voice heard. Other countries listened and, eventually, the President's corruption was exposed and he was removed from office. Wangari became Assistant Minister of the Environment, Natural Resources and Wildlife.

Wangari knew that when we plant a tree, we plant hope for the future. She also knew that tree conservation isn't only about putting more trees in the ground, it's about finding the right balance between woodland creation and restoration, between tree plantation and protection. And she knew that, when people come together in harmony, much can be achieved.

Community action

Community tree-planting initiatives are branching out in all corners of the world. Studies show that local people working together contributes to the success of tree-planting projects. So, why not start a community orchard, woodland or tree planting project of your own? Remember to factor in tree protection and maintenance too. You'll need to:

- Find the right location and get permission. Plant in historically forested but degraded areas if possible and avoid planting in peat. Find owners of local woodland and landowners and speak to your local council to find possible planting areas. Explain you will provide, plant and maintain the trees. One tree planted will absorb more than one ton of CO_2 in its lifetime and increase bird biodiversity by as much as 80 species. But it's important to plant the right trees at the right time in the right place. And be aware that post-planting, trees need aftercare too.
- Plant trees 2.5 metres apart during the tree-planting season (between October and February). Avoid planting close to walls or where underground cabling exists.
- Use tree guards (preferably non-plastic) and stakes to guide their growth and protect saplings from deer, rabbits and other wildlife.

- Prevent the risk of disease by ensuring saplings are home-grown rather than imported.
- Research to find out which trees are native to your area.
- Plant a diverse mixture of native trees to maximize their chance of long-term survival. Aim to recreate a natural habitat rather than planting uniform rows of the same species, which reduces the survival rate.
- Keep the trees weed-free for two to three years.
- Plant a shrubby understory (e.g., Goat Willow, Rowan, Hazel) alongside standards such as Oak, Field Maple and Wild Cherry. Find out which trees are native via your national forestry association.
- With permission, plant hedgerows and wildflower field margins that support all-important bee and insect corridors, which link up pollinators.

Or you could join a local rewilding or woodland regeneration project. Encouraging trees to self-seed and spread naturally avoids the need for planting yet creates new woodland. Natural regeneration may involve numerous approaches, including retaining Hawthorn and Blackberry scrub to protect fallen seedlings from animals, controlling grazing, ground-preparation work and direct seeding activities.

Hopeful Action

Dr Jane Goodall, primatologist and anthropologist, speaks in *The Book of Hope*, of four reasons for having hope when it comes to tackling the sometimes seemingly insurmountable obstacle of the climate crisis:

1. the amazing human intellect
2. the resilience of nature
3. the power of young people
4. the indomitable human spirit

Indeed, human intellect and spirit are creating some great initiatives that, together with nature's own resilience, can make a positive impact.

From carbon capture and storage (CCS) technologies to renewable-energy-powered zero-waste businesses that recycle resources; from community forester initiatives where volunteers across the globe plant trees and grow communities to citizen science projects that support tree health monitoring. From the production of sustainable Lego made from plant-based bioplastic sourced from sugar cane to T-shirts and crayons made from captured-carbon materials. Despite the destruction, much is being done to redress the balance, to hopefully aid the planet's recovery before it's too late.

> "Hope does not deny all the difficulty and all the danger that exists, but it is not stopped by them. There is a lot of darkness, but our actions create the light."
>
> **DR JANE GOODALL**

A decade ago, when my daughter was just four, her Forest School was one of a small but growing number in the UK. There are now hundreds across the country as antidotes to learning within the four walls of indoor classrooms, and the movement is growing internationally, enabling children to learn outdoors in nature, cook round campfires, whittle wood and play forest games. This offers hope that children, as a result of fostering a connection to nature through outdoor learning, may become committed stewards of the environment.

According to HRH Prince William, whose Earthshot Prize is rewarding those giving nature a helping hand to heal, "The natural world can return with vigour if we choose to protect it, and in return will protect us."

Earthshot Prize finalist, Tom Crowther, has an app called Restor, which helps anyone anywhere bring back biodiversity to the land by providing a kind of Google maps for nature. Instead of seeing restaurants dotted around the map, you see conservation initiatives. The app also provides information such as which native species to plant and predictions about how much carbon rewilding projects can capture. The goal of Restor

is to connect an international network of local environmentalists and restoration projects with one another, so they needn't work alone, and to connect a network of local sustainable projects with funders, governments and consumers. This could increase the impact of restoration projects across the globe by creating "an economically sustainable, global restoration movement."

Meanwhile, scientists are working hard to find alternatives to agricultural products that are causing the most forest damage. For example, plant geneticists are seeking alternatives for palm oil, the harvesting of which has devastating consequences, wiping out vast hectares of the Amazon rainforest annually. Algae might be one potential option, as some species, such as Chloridium can be made into a biocrude oil, which might be distillable as a diesel, jet fuel and heavy shipping oil replacement.

While the science proves that the number one priority to reverse the climate crisis and reduce global warming is to stop burning fossil fuels, all initiatives and solutions are worth pursuing while we continue to persuade the powers that be that fossil fuels should be phased out.

Global Solutions

When entire nations establish ways to serve the planet, it offers real hope. Take Bhutan, for example, the first and only country to become not just carbon neutral but carbon negative!

In the small Himalayan country, located between two of the worst polluters, China and India, greenhouse gas pollution is offset by extensive forests that sequester three times as much CO_2 as the country produces. It also sources electricity via hydropower from its many rapid-flowing rivers, and exports much of its renewable energy to India. *And* Bhutan banned logging exports in 1999, and has even written the protection of forest cover, currently at 80 per cent, into its constitution, ensuring it never falls below 60 per cent.

I first wrote about Bhutan in my book, *The Happiness Bible* because, rather than measure the success of its nation via Gross Domestic Product (GDP), Bhutan does so based on the wellbeing level of its citizens using a Gross National Happiness (GNH) index, a concept first introduced in 1972. Such harmonious balance between the wellness of people, environmental sustainability and economic growth offers a metric of success we can all aspire to. Bhutan is a shining example of what is possible when environmental sustainability and the mutual wellbeing of the natural world and its people is prioritized by a government.

The EU, whose consumption between 1990 and 2008 was responsible for 10 per cent of global deforestation, has drafted proposals for a new law banning the import of beef, palm oil, cocoa and other products to protect endangered forests worldwide. Companies will need to prove their agricultural commodities are not linked to deforestation or forest degradation and can now be held accountable thanks to satellite monitoring and geolocation tracking. Such tracking has been made easier thanks to Norway, which has funded a satellite map of the world's tropical forests across 64 countries. Deforestation-tracking data can ensure forests are being managed and used sustainably.

Pakistan's Billion Tree Tsunami project completed its goal of restoring 350,000 hectares of forest ahead of time, contributing to the Bonn Challenge which involves 59 countries committing land to reforestation by 2030.

And two of the biggest tree-planting efforts in history saw 800,000 women from Uttar Pradesh in India plant 50.4 million trees across 6,000 locations and 80 species in 24 hours. While the President of Ethiopia declared a public holiday in 2020 so everyone would plant trees, leading to 352 million trees being planted in Ethiopia in a single day!

The cloning of ancient stumps has offered hope for future forests too, with a "super grove" of 75 endangered Redwood Trees planted in California by non-profit group, Archangel Ancient Tree Archive, which creates "living libraries of old-growth tree genetics".

And urban centres are getting involved too, with numerous cities transforming old motorways and railways into green spaces and wild places, with walkways and green corridors being built in all corners of the globe, from Seoul and Singapore to Chicago and Philadelphia.

Of course, alongside national and local government initiatives, many conservation charities across the world continue to push reforestation agendas. For example, three of the biggest hitters in the world of international conservation – the World Wildlife Fund, BirdLife International and Wildlife Conservation Society – have come together to create the Trillion Trees programme, which aims to protect and restore a trillion trees by 2050. And in 2020 in the UK, the popular TV programme *Countryfile* launched "Plant Britain", a tree-planting campaign with an initial goal of planting 750,000 trees in two years - one for every child in the UK who started primary school that year.

Economical & Ecological Solutions

Evidently, across the world, people are uniting to plant and protect trees, but there is still a long way to go because the balance between economic necessity and ecological preservation is not a simple issue to fix, as the situation in British Columbia, Canada illustrates (see page 156). The good news is balanced solutions *are* possible, as the following initiatives demonstrate.

The Forest Garden Solution

Trees for the Future's Forest Garden Solution offers both hope and income for communities around the world by improving crop yields and watershed protection via reforestation. The initiative trains smallholder farmers in Sub-Saharan Africa to regenerate their land by swapping damaging agricultural practices with more fruitful ecologically and economically sound ones. Over four years the farmers learn to diversify their fields by planting and harvesting fast-growing fruit trees, which replenish the soil with nutrients and provide access to food plus increased income, even in the first year.

Costa Rica

Another Earthshot Prize winner, Costa Rica, actually *pays* people to preserve their ecosystem. Forest engineers teach locals how to manage their land and which crops and forests can grow side by side. This initiative has already doubled forest cover in just 25 years and gives local people an income.

Agroforestry

In the UK, agroforestry approaches are helping turn farmers into foresters. A combination of agriculture and forestry, agroforestry involves integrating trees with field crops and/or livestock. By diversifying planting fruit trees interspersed with arable crops, farmers can lengthen employment over extended seasons and expand and diversify food production, offering an economical incentive for this more environmentally friendly practice. Given that farmland covers 72 per cent of the British countryside, a move toward agroforestry could support the country's net-zero carbon emissions target.

Menominee Forest

In Wisconsin, the success of the Menominee Forest shows it's possible to balance ecology with economy. It has profitably harvested twice the forest's volume (over 2 billion board feet) over the past 150 years yet, today, *more* trees stand than when logging began.

This has been achieved by maintaining an old and diverse growing stock, with trees being allowed to age to become 200-plus-year-old grandmother trees. Lower-quality, ailing trees are removed to make space for others to grow larger and healthier.

The Mission Green project

Dr Meg Lowman, the first person to study trees from the canopy, founded Mission Green to provide a sustainable economic incentive opportunity for local people by building canopy walkways in endangered forests across the world as aerial-trail tourist attractions. These attractions empower Indigenous communities to earn a living from eco-tourism – as guides, lodge operators, drivers, cooks and trail builders – rather than from palm oil or other destructive agriculture. And it's working – one of Mission Green's walkways in Malaysia, which has already given 30 local people permanent jobs, has been honoured as a UNESCO World Heritage biological site, so will be conserved in perpetuity.

Mission Green also intends to fund student fellowships to document biodiversity and create a pipeline of experts in the next generation, for education is also vital.

Reciprocation is Good

Engaging in tree-positive initiatives, exploring and discovering more about trees, and stepping off the hedonic treadmill can all motivate us to refocus our attention away from the fallacy of "I'll be happy when …" toward the beauty of what we already have to be grateful for, namely, trees.

EDUCATION

Learning about trees and environmental change, then sharing your knowledge to educate others, is a great way to serve trees:

- Support research projects by getting involved in Citizen Science research and monitoring projects. Learn how to identify tree pests and diseased trees so you can help gather important data and report issues to protect more trees.
- Find out about sustainable forestry, which considers consequences of actions in relation to the whole ecosystem.
- Spread the word about the value of trees and the concept of balanced harmonious action by writing blogs and articles, posting on social media and talking to friends, family, teachers, students, local businesses and community groups.
- Take a course to qualify in an ecological profession – be that sustainable forestry, agroforestry, permaculture, eco-planning or biophilic design.

If trees could talk they would educate us. I asked Peter Wohlleben, author of *The Hidden Life of Trees*, what he thought trees would say if they could talk. Peter told me, "If trees could talk to us they would warn us about what we are doing. They are working hard to keep stable environment conditions, but people are always disturbing their systems. So they would ask us to be more gentle."

Trees (unfortunately) cannot talk to us, –but we can talk to them. And I think the first thing we should say to them is "Thank you."

Thanksgiving

"As you walk upon the
sacred earth, treat each
step as a prayer."

BLACK ELK

From the gospel songs of African-Americans to the Thanksgiving Address of Indigenous tribes, from the praiseful psalms of Ancient Hebrews to the grateful Haiku of the Japanese, when we honour what is all around us, we see it more clearly and brightly and find the light that we seek.

I want to end this book as it began, with appreciation; to start and end with gratitude, just as our days ought to.

As children, when given a gift, we're taught it's polite to say thank you. But how often do we thank trees for what they give us?

For as long as they can remember, parents of the Mohawk tribe have taught their children to start each day with their traditional Thanksgiving Address. When you start each day with gratitude to Mother Earth you notice the gifts she provides as precious, and you savour them.

In the Haudenosaunee Confederacy (see page 154), the Thanksgiving Address is known as *Ohenten Kariwatekwen*, which translates as "words spoken before all others" and expresses how words of gratitude and respect are prioritized. This brief extract speaks of the interconnectedness between us all, how we are meant to live in harmony with each other, and our gratitude and respect for gifts so generously given.

"Beginning with where our feet first touch the earth, we send greetings and thanks to all members of the natural world."

"We have been given the duty to live in balance and harmony with each other and all living things ... so now let us bring our minds together as one as we give greetings and thanks to each other as People. Now our minds are one."

"To our Mother, we send thanksgiving, love and respect ... "

"Standing around us we see all the Trees. The Earth has many families of Trees who each have their own instructions and uses. Some provide shelter and shade, others fruit and beauty and many useful gifts. The Maple is the leader of the trees, to recognize its gift of sugar when the People need it most. Many peoples of the world recognize a Tree as a symbol of peace and strength. With one mind we greet and thank the Tree life. Now our minds are one."

Addressing Trees with Thanks

Humans are the only living creatures who have the capacity for gratitude, and it's important to use this unique gift. The more we count our blessings, the more blessings we notice. And when we stop taking trees' gifts for granted and respond with gratitude through restorative action, trees reply to our thanks with more gifts, and with love.

- Thank the trees in your Treestory for being part of your life. Thank each individual tree for what it's given you; for how it's made you feel good.

- Thank the trees of the world for what they've gifted you, e.g., *"Thank you trees for the air I breathe, the home I live in, the floor I walk on, the food I eat, the chair I sit on, the pencil and paper I write with, the medicine I heal myself with, the books I read. Your breath is my breath and my breath is yours."*

- Write out the Thanksgiving Address extract (see above), perhaps in calligraphy or on a piece of artwork you've painted. Forage for twigs and leaves to border your word art, and frame it with wood.

Conclusion

"Reciprocity is a key to success.
What we contemplate here is more
than ecological restoration; it is
the restoration of relationship
between plants and people."

ROBIN WALL KIMMERER,
BRAIDING SWEETGRASS

Somewhere a child picks a mango from a tree, while elsewhere an office-worker eats their lunch beneath one. Trees of all shapes, sizes and species link us together.

Across lifespans, they stand in a vast collective of loving kindness in all they gift us and a deep knowing in all they can teach us.

Trees' scents and sights are imprinted deep into our memories from long ago, making us remember. They provide the backdrop to our present on this forested earth and offer hope for our future.

And as I stand in the forest, I'm reminded how transformative tree glee can be when we reconnect to our evolutionary biology and psychology, tune in to our senses and feel gratitude for their arboreal abundance.

From sapling to Broad Oak, from garden to rainforest, from preservation to propagation, it's up to us to renew our covenant with the trees that our ancestors once had and Indigenous people never lost.

Loving the natural world so deeply in this way feels good and does good. Loving trees activates us to protect and celebrate them.

For forests and for humanity the best way forward is in unity. Trees teach us this. I hope this book has revealed the significance and the personhood of trees as more than scenery or a commodity, but integral – not just to our life on Earth – but to our life satisfaction and wellness. Let us see trees as "Standing People" who are part of an important fellowship, so we may work together in partnership.

Let's be done with the tyranny of self-important species' supremacy, which places humans atop the hierarchy. In seeing trees standing alongside us not as "things" but as "beings", as extended family, moving from objectification and subjectification toward personification, may we develop greater empathy and responsibility.

All species on Earth are united in their desire to survive, to live. And we all want the best for our young – be we tree or humankind, animal or organism, this desire links us all.

Trees can show us the way. They remember what we've forgotten. Trees model resilience, patience and balance, flexibility, stillness and generosity. And, most of all, they model what relationship looks like; what love feels like. Trees are kin and trees are kind.

It's not (yet) too late. There is hope. We can rekindle our romance with trees and restore our relationship by following their lead.

May your attention lead to intention, taking you from noticing in awe and wonder to noting and sharing and responding with restorative action. May this book, my own testimony to trees, which I acknowledge is written with love

and gratitude on their bodies, be an act of reciprocity in itself – a reminder – to value the treasures of tree glee and to appreciate, connect and reciprocate with our oldest companions.

I hope these pages have explained how and why trees make us feel restored, reassured, revitalized, reconnected and respectful; how they make us feel better and how mutually restorative tree glee can be. May this book plant a seed within you to deepen your own personal relationship with trees.

I hope you've seen how the more time we spend in trees' company, the more we can restore balance, not only to the planet's ecosystem, but to our own; how we can find our own truth in trees and connect more deeply to ourselves as we connect more deeply with them.

Placing their best interests in our hearts, we can thrive together and mutually flourish in balanced harmony and cherished community.

As trees' branches continue to frame our lives as we grow together, as we write the next chapters of our treestories, let us remember our reciprocal love and light each other up.

Useful Resources

Amazon Sacred Headwaters: www.
sacredheadwaters.org

American Forests National Big Tree
Program: www.americanforests.
org/get-involved/americas-biggest-
trees/champion-trees-national-
register

Ancient Forest Alliance:
www.ancientforestalliance.org

Ancient Tree Inventory:
https://ati.woodlandtrust.org.uk/add-
a-tree

Ancient wood finder: www.magic.gov.uk

Arbor Day Foundation:
www.arborday.org

Australian Government Forestry:
www.awe.gov.au/agriculture-land/
forestry

Become a tree warden:
www.treecouncil.org.uk

Canopy Planet: www.canopyplanet.org

Charter for Trees, Woods and People:
www.treecharter.uk

Earthwatch: www.earthwatch.org

Forestry Commission England:
www.forestryengland.uk

Forest Stewardship Council: www.fsc.org

Global Monumental Tree Record:
www.monumentaltrees.com

International Tree Foundation:
www.internationaltreefoundation.org

Mission Green: www.mission-green.org

Mother Tree Project:
www.mothertreeproject.org

National Trust Plant a Tree:
www.nationaltrust.org.uk/features/
plant-a-tree

The Nature Conservancy:
www.nature.org

One Tree Planted:
www.onetreeplanted.org

The Outdoor Guide:
www.theoutdoorguide.co.uk

Plant a Tree Today Foundation:
www.pattfoundation.org

Plant Britain: www.plantbritain.co.uk

The Queen's Green Canopy:
www.queensgreencanopy.org

Rainforest Action Network:
https://act.ran.org/

Restor: www.restor.eco

Tree Glee website – read more tree
tales: www.treeglee.co.uk

Tree-planting platform:
www.moretrees.eco

Tree-planting search engine:
www.ecosia.org

Trees For Cities: www.treesforcities.org

Trillion Trees: www.trilliontrees.org

US Forestry Service: www.fs.usda.gov

Woodland Trust:
www.woodlandtrust.org.uk

Woodland Trust's Nature Calendar:
https://naturescalendar.
woodlandtrust.org.uk/
media/1817/10103-natures-calendar-
date-range-poster.pdf

Endnotes

Chapter 1

1   Ideno Y, Hayashi K, Abe Y, et al. "Blood pressure-lowering effect of Shinrin-yoku (Forest bathing): a systematic review and meta-analysis." *BMC Complementary and Alternative Medicine*. 2017;17(1):409. Published 2017 Aug 16. doi: 10.1186/s12906-017-1912-z.

2   Li Q, Kobayashi M, Wakayama Y, Inagaki H, Katsumata M, Hirata Y, Hirata K, Shimizu T, Kawada T, Park B J, Ohira T, Kagawa T, Miyazaki Y. "Effect of phytoncide from trees on human natural killer cell function." *International Journal of Immunopathology and Pharmacology*. 2009 Oct-Dec;22(4):951-9. doi: 10.1177/039463200902200410.

3   Li Q, "Effect of forest bathing trips on human immune function." *Environmental Health and Preventative Medicine*. 2010;15(1):9-17. doi: 10.1007/s12199-008-0068-3

4   Li Q, Morimoto K, Nakadai A, Inagaki H, Katsumata M, Shimizu T, Hirata Y, Hirata K, Suzuki H, Miyazaki Y, Kagawa T, Koyama Y, Ohira T, Takayama N, Krensky AM, Kawada T. "Forest bathing enhances human natural killer activity and expression of anti-cancer proteins." *International Journal of Immunopathology and Pharmacology*. 2007 Apr-Jun;20(2 Suppl 2):3-8. doi: 10.1177/03946320070200S202.

5   Reid C E, Clougherty J E, Shmool J L C, Kubzansky L D. "Is All Urban Green Space the Same? A Comparison of the Health Benefits of Trees and Grass in New York City." *International Journal of Environmental Research and Public Health*. 2017; 14(11):1411. doi: 10.3390/ijerph14111411.

6   Won Sop Shin. "The influence of forest view through a window on job satisfaction and job stress." *Scandinavian Journal of Forest Research*. 2007; 22:3, 248-253, doi: 10.1080/02827580701262733.

7   Marselle M R, Bowler D E, Watzema J et al. "Urban street tree biodiversity and antidepressant prescriptions." *Scientific Reports* 10, 22445 (2020). doi: 10.1038/s41598-020-79924-5.

8   Ward Thompson C, Roe J, Aspinall P, Mitchell R, Clow A, Miller D. "More green space is linked to less stress in deprived communities: Evidence from salivary cortisol patterns." *Landscape and Urban Planning*. Volume 105, Issue 3, 2012, Pages 221-229, ISSN 0169-2046, doi: 10.1016/j.landurbplan.2011.12.015.

9   Oh SU, Kim E-H, Kim K-M, Kim M-K. "A Study on the Application of Successful Forest Greening Experience for Forest and Landscape Restoration: A Comparative Study of Two Koreas." *Sustainability*. 2020; 12(20):8712. doi: 10.3390/su12208712.

10 Hammoud R, Tognin S, Bakolis I, et al. "Lonely in a crowd: investigating the association between overcrowding and loneliness using smartphone technologies." *Scientific Reports* 11, 24134 (2021). doi: 10.1038/s41598-021-03398-2.

11 Lee J, Tsunetsugu Y, Takayama N, Park BJ, Li Q, Song C, Komatsu M, Ikei H, Tyrväinen L, Kagawa T, Miyazaki Y. "Influence of forest therapy on cardiovascular relaxation in young adults." *Evidence-Based Complementary and Alternative Medicine.* 2014;2014:834360. doi: 10.1155/2014/834360.

12 Marselle M R, Warber S L, Irvine K N. "Growing Resilience through Interaction with Nature: Can Group Walks in Nature Buffer the Effects of Stressful Life Events on Mental Health?" *International Journal of Environmental Research and Public Health.* 2019 Mar 19;16(6):986. doi: 10.3390/ijerph16060986.

13 Park B J, Tsunetsugu Y, Kasetani T et al. "The physiological effects of Shinrin-yoku (taking in the forest atmosphere or forest bathing): evidence from field experiments in 24 forests across Japan." *Environmental Health and Preventative Medicine* 15, 18 (2010). doi: 10.1007/s12199-009-0086-9.

14 Bielinis E, Omelan A, Boiko S and Bielinis L. "The Restorative Effect of Staying in a Broad-Leaved Forest on Healthy Young Adults in Winter and Spring." *Baltic Forestry.* 2019. 24(2): 218-227.

15 Kenny R. "A critical exploration of the role of the learning disposition 'resilience' in the learning and development of young children." 2010. http://www.academia.edu/541952/A_critical_exploration_of_the_role_of_the_learning_disposition_resilience_in_the_learning_and_development_of_young_children

16 Persil. "Dirt Is Good" project. 2016. www.dirtisgood.com/uk/truth-about-dirt.html.

17 Taylor A F, Kuo F E, Sullivan W C. "Coping with ADD: The Surprising Connection to Green Play Settings." *Environment and Behavior.* 2001;33(1):54-77. doi: 10.1177/00139160121972864.

18 www.independent.co.uk/life-style/health-and-families/features/when-we-stop-children-taking-risks-do-we-stunt-their-emotional-growth-9422057.html.

19 Richardson M et al. "The Impact of Children's Connection to Nature: A Report for the Royal Society for the Protection of Birds (RSPB)." Royal Society for the Protection of Birds. 2016. Available at: www.rspb.org.uk/our-work/our-positions-and-campaigns/positions/education/research/connection-to-nature.aspx.

20 Maher B A, Ahmed I A M, Davison B, Karloukovski V, and Clarke R. "Impact of Roadside Tree Lines on Indoor Concentrations of Traffic-Derived Particulate Matter." *Environmental Science & Technology.* 2013 47 (23), 13737-13744. doi: 10.1021/es404363m.

Chapter 2

21 Aspinall P, Mavros P, Coyne R, Roe J. "The urban brain: analysing outdoor physical activity with mobile EEG." *British Journal of Sports Medicine.* 2015 Feb;49(4):272-6. doi: 10.1136/bjsports-2012-091877.

22 Li, Dr Qing, *Into the Forest: How Trees Can Help You Find Health and Happiness,* Penguin Life (2019).

23 Morita E, Imai M, Okawa M, Miyaura T, Miyazaki S. "A before and after comparison

of the effects of forest walking on the sleep of a community-based sample of people with sleep complaints." *BioPsychoSocial Medicine*. 2011;5:13. Published 2011 Oct 14. doi: 10.1186/1751-0759-5-13.

24 Ulrich R S, Simons R F, Losito B D, Fiorito E, Miles M A and Zelson M. . "Stress recovery during exposure to natural and urban environments." *Journal of Environmental Psychology*. 1991 11(3), 201–230. doi: 10.1016/S0272-4944(05)80184-7.

25 Ulrich R S. "View through a window may influence recovery from surgery." *Science*. 1984 Apr 27;224(4647):420-1. doi: 10.1126/science.6143402.

26 Kang Y & Kim E J. "Differences of Restorative Effects While Viewing Urban Landscapes and Green Landscapes." *Sustainability*. 2019; 11(7):2129. doi: 10.3390/su11072129.

27 Ulrich R S, Simons R F, Losito B D, Fiorito E, Miles M A and Zelson M. "Stress recovery during exposure to natural and urban environments." *Journal of Environmental Psychology*. 1991 11(3), 201–230. doi: 10.1016/S0272-4944(05)80184-7.

28 Tyrväinen L, Ojala A, Korpela K, Lanki T, Tsunetsugu Y, Kagawa T. "The influence of urban green environments on stress relief measures: A field experiment." *Journal of Environmental Psychology*. Volume 38, 2014, Pages 1-9, ISSN 0272-4944, doi: 10.1016/j.jenvp.2013.12.005.

29 Berman M G et al. "Interacting with Nature Improves Cognition and Affect for Individals with Depression." *Journal of Affective Disorders*. 2012 Nov; 140(3): 300–305. doi: 10.1016/j.jad.2012.03.012.

30 Atchley R A, Strayer D L, Atchley P. "Creativity in the Wild: Improving Creative Reasoning through Immersion in Natural Settings." *PLoS ONE*. 2012. 7(12): e51474. doi: 10.1371/journal.pone.0051474

31 Fredrickson, Barbara, *Positivity: Groundbreaking Research to Release Your Inner Optimist and Thrive*, Oneworld Publications (2011).

32 Atchley P & Lane S. "Chapter Four - Cognition in the Attention Economy." Editor: Brian H. Ross, *Psychology of Learning and Motivation*, Academic Press, Volume 61, 2014, Pages 133-177, ISSN 0079-7421, ISBN 9780128002834, doi: 10.1016/B978-0-12-800283-4.00004-6.

33 Basu A, Duvall J, Kaplan R. "Attention Restoration Theory: Exploring the Role of Soft Fascination and Mental Bandwidth." *Environment and Behavior*. 2018; 51(9-10):1055-1081. doi: 10.1177/0013916518774400.

34 Hopman R J, LoTemplio S B , Scott E E et al. "Resting-state posterior alpha power changes with prolonged exposure in a natural environment." *Cognitive Research*. 5, 51 (2020). doi: 10.1186/s41235-020-00247-0.

35 Kobayashi H, Ikei H, Song C, Kagawa T, Miyazaki Y. "Comparing the impact of forest walking and forest viewing on psychological states." *Urban Forestry & Urban Greening*. Volume 57, 2021, 126920, ISSN 1618-8667, doi: 10.1016/j.ufug.2020.126920.

Chapter 3

36 https://blogs.uoregon.edu/richardtaylor/2016/02/03/human-physiological-responses-to-fractals-in-nature-and-art.

37 Wilkins, Prof. Arnold. "Disturbing Vision." TedxUniversityofEssex, https://youtu.be/GBOzv9HgoWM?t=5s.

38 Rybczynski, Witold, *A Clearing in the Distance: Frederick Law Olmsted and North America in the Nineteenth Century*, Scribner (2000).

39 Akers A, Barton J, Cossey R, Gainsford P, Griffin M, Micklewright D. "Visual color perception in green exercise: positive effects on mood and perceived exertion." *Environmental Science & Technology*. 2012 Aug 2;46(16):8661-6. doi: 10.1021/es301685g.

40 Kurt S & Osueke K K. "The Effects of Color on the Moods of College Students." *SAGE Open*. Februuary 2014. doi: 10.1177/2158244014525423.

41 Mammarella N, Di Domenico A, Palumbo R, Fairfield B. "When green iş positive and red is negative: Aging and the influence of color on emotional memories." *Psychology and Aging*. 2016;31(8):914-926. doi: 10.1037/pag0000122.

42 Stringer J, Donald G. "Aromasticks in cancer care: an innovation not to be sniffed at." *Complementary Therapies in Clinical Practice*. 2011 May;17(2):116-21. doi: 10.1016/j.ctcp.2010.06.002.

43 Salehi B, Upadhyay S, Erdogan Orhan I, et al. "Therapeutic Potential of α- and β-Pinene: A Miracle Gift of Nature." *Biomolecules*. 2019;9(11):738. doi: 10.3390/biom9110738.

44 Annerstedt M, Jönsson P, Wallergård M, Johansson G, Karlson B, Grahn P, Hansen AM, Währborg P. "Inducing physiological stress recovery with sounds of nature in a virtual reality forest – results from a pilot study." *Physiology & Behavior*. 2013 Jun 13;118:240-50. doi: 10.1016/j.physbeh.2013.05.023.

45 Gould van Praag C, Garfinkel S, Sparasci O et al. "Mind-wandering and alterations to default mode network connectivity when listening to naturalistic versus artificial sounds." *Scientific Reports* 7, 45273 (2017). doi: 10.1038/srep45273.

46 https://www.soulveda.com/wellbeing/a-chirping-tweet-for-the-day.

Chapter 4

47 Lyubomirsky, Sonja, *The How of Happiness*, Piatkus (2010).

48 Phelps C, Butler C, Cousins A, Hughes C. "Sowing the seeds or failing to blossom? A feasibility study of a simple ecotherapy-based intervention in women affected by breast cancer." *Ecancermedicalscience*. 2015;9:602. Published 2015 Dec 1. doi: 10.3332/ecancer.2015.602

49 Zhang J W, Howell R T, Iyer R. "Engagement with Natural Beauty Moderates the Positive Relation between Connectedness with Nature and Psychological Well-Being." *Journal of Environmental Psychology*. (2014). Volume 38, 2014, Pages 55-63, ISSN 0272-4944, doi: 10.1016/j.jenvp.2013.12.013.

50 Piff P K, Dietze P, Feinberg M, Stancato D M and Keltner D. "Awe, the small self, and prosocial behavior." *Journal of Personality and Social Psychology.* 2015, 108(6), 883–899. doi: 10.1037/pspi0000018.

51 Davis, Nora, Ph.D., *The Role of Transcendent Nature and Awe Experiences on Positive Environmental Engagement,* University of California, Irvine (2016).

52 Zhang J W, Piff P K, Iyer R, Koleva S and Keltner D. "An occasion for unselfing: Beautiful nature leads to prosociality." *Journal of Environmental Psychology.* 2014, 37, 61–72. doi: 10.1016/j.jenvp.2013.11.008.

53 Piff P K, Dietze P, Feinberg M, Stancato D M and Keltner D. "Awe, the small self, and prosocial behavior." *Journal of Personality and Social Psychology.* 2015, 108(6), 883–899. doi: 10.1037/pspi0000018.

54 Rudd M, Vohs KD, Aaker J. "Awe expands people's perception of time, alters decision making, and enhances well-being". *Psychological Science.* 2012 Oct 1;23(10):1130-6. doi: 10.1177/0956797612438731.

55 McCraty R & Childre D. "The Grateful Heart: The Psychophysiology of Appreciation." In Emmons R A and McCullough M E (Eds.), *The Psychology of Gratitude,* Oxford University Press (2004); pp. 230–255.

56 Wong YJ, Owen J, Gabana NT, Brown JW, McInnis S, Toth P, Gilman L. "Does gratitude writing improve the mental health of psychotherapy clients? Evidence from a randomized controlled trial." *Psychotherapy Research.* 2018 Mar;28(2):192-202. doi: 10.1080/10503307.2016.1169332.

57 Martin L, White M P, Hunt A, Richardson M, Pahl S and Burt J. "Nature contact, nature connectedness and associations with health, wellbeing and pro-environmental behaviours." *Journal of Environmental Psychology.* Volume 68, 2020, 101389, ISSN 0272-4944. doi: 10.1016/j.jenvp.2020.101389.

58 https://www.johnmuirtrust.org/resources/788-wild-and-well-nature-connection-wellbeing-and-meaning-in-life.

59 Ryan R M, Weinstein N, Bernstein J, Brown K W, Mistretta L, Gagné M. "Vitalizing effects of being outdoors and in nature." *Journal of Environmental Psychology.* Volume 30, Issue 2, 2010, Pages 159-168, ISSN 0272-4944. doi: 10.1016/j.jenvp.2009.10.009.

60 *Ecotherapy:The Green Agenda for Mental Health* (2007) Mind.

61 Buckley RC, Brough P. "Nature, Eco, and Adventure Therapies for Mental Health and Chronic Disease." *Frontiers in Public Health.* 2017 Aug 21;5:220. doi: 10.3389/fpubh.2017.00220.

62 Summary Report from Good from Woods Partners, www.plymouth.ac.uk/uploads/production/document/path/7/7981/summary-report-foat-shirelink-3.pdf.

Chapter 5

63 Simard, Suzanne, *Finding the Mother Tree: Uncovering the Wisdom and Intelligence of the Forest,* Allen Lane (2021).

64 Seery MD, Holman EA, Silver RC. "Whatever does not kill us: cumulative lifetime adversity, vulnerability, and resilience." *Journal of Personality and Social Psychology.* 2010 Dec;99(6):1025-41. doi: 10.1037/a0021344.

65 Seligman, Martin, *Flourish: A New Understanding of Happiness and Wellbeing*, Nicholas Brealey Publishing (2011).

66 Kleim B, Ehlers A. "Evidence for a curvilinear relationship between posttraumatic growth and posttrauma depression and PTSD in assault survivors." *Journal of Traumatic Stress*. 2009 Feb;22(1):45-52. doi: 10.1002/jts.20378.

Chapter 6

67 Richardson M & Sheffield D. "Reflective self-attention: A more stable predictor of connection to nature than mindful attention." *Ecopsychology*. Sep 2015 7(3).166-175.doi: 10.1089/eco.2015.0010.

68 Howell A J, Dopko R L, Passmore H-A, Buro K. "Nature connectedness: Associations with well-being and mindfulness." *Personality and Individual Differences*. Volume 51, Issue 2, 2011, Pages 166-171, ISSN 0191-8869, doi: 10.1016/j.paid.2011.03.037.

69 Richardson M & Sheffield D. "Reflective self-attention: A more stable predictor of connection to nature than mindful attention." *Ecopsychology*. Sep 2015 7(3).166-175.doi: 10.1089/eco.2015.0010.

70 Mayer F S, Frantz C M, Bruehlman-Senecal E, Dolliver K. "Why Is Nature Beneficial?: The Role of Connectedness to Nature." *Environment and Behavior*. 2009;41(5):607-643. doi: 10.1177/0013916508319745.

71 Richardson M & Sheffield D. "Three good things in nature: Noticing nearby nature brings sustained increases in connection with nature." *Psyecology*. 2017; 8 (1). pp. 1-32. doi: 10.1080/21711976.2016.1267136.

Chapter 7

72 Fivush R, Duke M, Bohanek J G. "'Do You Know...' The power of family history in adolescent identity and well-being." University of North Carolina (Chapel Hill), February 2010.

Chapter 9

73 Pink, Daniel H, *Drive: The Surprising Truth About What Motivates Us*, Cannongate (2010).

74 Morton C, Trenholm R, Beukema S (ESSA Technologies), Botd R, Knowler D. "Economic Valuation of Old-Growth Forests on Vancouver Island. Ancient Forest Alliance." Simon Fraser University. 2021. www.ancientforestalliance.org/old-growth-economic-report.

Chapter 10

75 London Assembly publication. "Chainsaw massacre: A review of London's street trees." 2007. www.london.gov.uk/about-us/london-assembly/london-assembly-publications/chainsaw-massacre-review-londons-street-trees.

Picture Credits